STUDIES IN POPULATION

STUDIES IN POPULATION

Proceedings of the Annual Meeting of the
Population Association of America
at Princeton, New Jersey
May 1949

EDITED BY GEORGE F. MAIR

PRINCETON, NEW JERSEY
PRINCETON UNIVERSITY PRESS
1949

COPYRIGHT, 1949, BY PRINCETON UNIVERSITY PRESS
LONDON: GEOFFREY CUMBERLEGE, OXFORD UNIVERSITY PRESS

PRINTED IN THE UNITED STATES OF AMERICA

PREFACE

This volume is an experiment. In past years, with no provision made for the publication of the papers read at meetings of the Population Association of America, much material potentially useful to demographers and workers in associated fields was never put into print. Believing that a remedy for this situation might be desirable and that the 1949 annual meeting included papers of considerable quality and interest, the Executive Committee of the Association requested the Office of Population Research to arrange for publication of the proceedings of the meeting in some suitable but relatively inexpensive form. The present volume is the outcome. It is intended not only to make the papers and discussion more widely available, but to obtain an indication of the extent of existing interest in publications of this sort.

The five sections that follow correspond to the five sessions of the meeting, and include two on current problems and techniques, one on resources, and two on fertility. As is often the case in demography, the subject matter is diverse and yet variously interrelated. In three instances, summaries are given instead of complete papers. Two of these papers are being published elsewhere; citation to the appropriate journal is given with the summary. One paper not presented at the meeting is included in the third section. Since the session on resources was designed to give the members of the Association an opportunity to hear discussions by specialists in fields other than population, it was thought that readers would be interested to have also a consideration of the subject from a specifically demographic point of view. Professor Warren S. Thompson, of the Scripps Foundation for Research in Population Problems, Miami University, has been kind enough to prepare such a paper especially for this volume.

The Program Committee for the 1949 annual meeting consisted of Rupert Vance, Chairman, Samuel C. Newman, and Christopher Tietze. They were assisted in planning the details of the meetings by the Chairmen of the several sessions.

The editor would like to express his gratitude to the authors represented herein for their ready cooperation and to his colleagues in the Office of Population Research for valuable assistance in preparing the book for publication. Particular thanks are due to Carla Adelt Sykes for her energetic and skillful attention to editorial and production problems.

George F. Mair, Editor

Office of Population Research
Princeton University
October, 1949

TABLE OF CONTENTS

	Page
Preface	v

SECTION I
Application of Demographic Data to Current Problems

Total Marital Dissolutions in the United States: Relative Importance of Mortality and Divorce
   Paul H. Jacobson, Metropolitan Life Insurance Company 3

Total Marital Dissolutions in the United States: Relative Importance of Mortality and Divorce: Discussion
   Samuel C. Newman, National Office of Vital Statistics 16

The Length of Working Life (Summary)
   Seymour L. Wolfbein, Bureau of Labor Statistics 17

The Length of Working Life: Discussion
   A.J. Jaffe, U. S. Bureau of the Census 19

Report on a Series of Illegal Abortions Induced by Physicians
   Christopher Tietze, M.D., National Committee on Maternal Health ... 21

SECTION II
Tools for Demographic Research

Our Current Demographic Inventory: Review of Data from the Current Population Survey (Summary)
   A. Ross Eckler, U. S. Bureau of the Census 29

Recent Proposals for Modifying the Net Reproduction Rate (Summary)
   T.J. Woofter, Jr., Federal Security Agency 32

Recent Proposals for Modifying the Net Reproduction Rate: Discussion
   John Hajnal, Population Division, United Nations 34

Washington's State-Wide System of Census Tracts and Census Divisions
   Calvin F. Schmid, University of Washington 39

Census Divisions in the State of Washington: Discussion
   Clarence E. Batschelet, U. S. Bureau of the Census 46

SECTION III
Resources for the World's People

Population and Scarce Food Resources
   John D. Black, Harvard University 51

Soil Resources and the World's Potential Food Supply
   Richard Bradfield, Cornell University 66

Management of Resources in the Tennessee Valley
  Gordon R. Clapp, Tennessee Valley Authority.......................... 77
Some Reflections on World Population and Food Supply during the
  Next Few Decades
  Warren S. Thompson, Miami University............................... 80

SECTION IV
Value Systems and Human Fertility

The Reproductive Mores of the Asian Peasant
  Irene B. Taeuber, Princeton University................................. 95
Demographic Values in the Middle Ages
  Josiah C. Russell, University of New Mexico.......................... 103
The Catholic Value System in Relation to Human Fertility
  Rev. William J. Gibbons, S.J... 108
Values, Population, and the Supernatural: A Critique
  Kingsley Davis, Columbia University.................................. 135

SECTION V
Future Course of Research in Fertility

Physiological Factors and Their Control
  Howard C. Taylor, Jr., M.D., Columbia University................... 143
An Approach to Research in Overcoming Cultural Barriers to
  Family Limitation
  Clarence Senior, Columbia University................................. 148
Needed Research on Fertility of Negroes
  Ira De A. Reid, Haverford College...................................... 153
The Future Course of Research in Fertility: Measures and Methods
  Wilson H. Grabill, U. S. Bureau of the Census....................... 157
Some Aspects of Research in Differential Fertility
  Ronald Freedman, University of Michigan............................ 161
The Psychiatric Approach to Research Interviewing
  Moya Woodside, Neurological Institute of New York................ 166

SECTION I

APPLICATION OF DEMOGRAPHIC DATA TO CURRENT PROBLEMS

Morning Session, May 28, 1949
Dorothy Swaine Thomas, University of Pennsylvania, Chairman

TOTAL MARITAL DISSOLUTIONS IN THE UNITED STATES: RELATIVE IMPORTANCE OF MORTALITY AND DIVORCE[1]

Paul H. Jacobson
Metropolitan Life Insurance Company

The abnormal trends in vital phenomena engendered by the war have stimulated a growing awareness of the need for detailed statistics on all phases of family life in our country. In the absence of data other than the annual number of marriages and divorces, undue emphasis has come to be placed on these crude statistics for interpreting what is happening to the American family. Recognizing this problem, the Bureau of the Census has recently expanded the scope of its sample surveys to include more detailed information on the family. For example, in its April 1948 survey, the Bureau collected information on the duration of present marital status and on the number of times married persons had been married—the first time such nation-wide figures were collected. The National Office of Vital Statistics has also expanded its activities in this field. For the present, however, its major emphasis is being directed toward encouraging and advising States in building centralized record systems so that comprehensive statistics could eventually be provided for an expanding area of the country.

Meanwhile, there remains an immediate need for detailed data on marriage and divorce, such as age, residence, previous marital status, duration of marriage, relative importance of dissolutions by mortality and divorce, and the number of children affected. This information is particularly needed for the war and immediate postwar period, and its absence cannot be remedied by data made available at any future date, such as by the 1950 Census or by registration data for subsequent years. It seemed desirable, therefore, to reconstruct the patterns of recent trends, even if this had to be estimated from statistics for only a handful of States. The present paper, developed on this basis, contains some findings on the trend of marital dissolutions in the United States, specifically the roles of mortality and divorce (including annulment), and the variation in dissolutions according to duration of marriage. Since it is not practical to present all of the details on the sources of the basic statistics, their limitations, and their representativeness, it should be emphasized that many of the findings are only approximations.

Trend of Divorce. In the United States, in 1948, there were about 11.7 divorces (or annulments) for every 1,000 married couples. This is one-sixth below the rate for 1947, and more than one-third under the all-time high of 18.5 in 1946. Although the frequency of divorce has declined sharply from its postwar peak, the rate in 1948 was still the fifth highest in our history, exceeding the rate for every year prior to 1944.

The long-term upward trend of the divorce rate is clearly evident from Figure 1, which shows the number of divorces granted per 1,000 married couples from 1867 to 1948.[2] The pattern is well known, and is fairly similar to the picture obtained by relating divorces to the total population, or to the number of marriages performed in the preceding ten years. As may be noted from the figure, the divorce rate has increased almost without interruption. In the years immediately after the Civil War, the rate was less than 2 per 1,000 married couples; by the beginning of World War I, it was about 5 per 1,000; and at the time of Pearl Harbor, it was almost 10 per 1,000. Three major deviations from trend occurred during the 80 years for which statistics are available. The first was recorded in 1920 when the rate rose to 7.8 per 1,000 couples; the second, during the depression, when the rate dropped to 6.1 in 1932 and 1933; and the third and most pronounced during World War II and the early postwar period.

Trend of Total Marital Dissolutions. This, in brief, is the picture of the trend of marital dissolutions in our country to which we have become accustomed, but it does not give us the complete pattern of what is happening to the American family. While legal dissolutions of marriage have been increasing in frequency for almost a century, the relative importance of dissolutions due to the death of either husband or wife has been decreasing for at least that length of time.

Willcox was probably the first American demographer who took cognizance of the fact that a marriage may end "naturally" by the death of either spouse or "civilly" by divorce or annulment.[3] He and a number of subsequent researchers considered the problem in terms of the relative importance of death and divorce, but only with a view toward estimating the probability that a marriage would end in divorce.[4] No one, apparently, has considered quantitatively the total effect on the family of the long-term upward trend of divorce and the downward course of mortality. What has

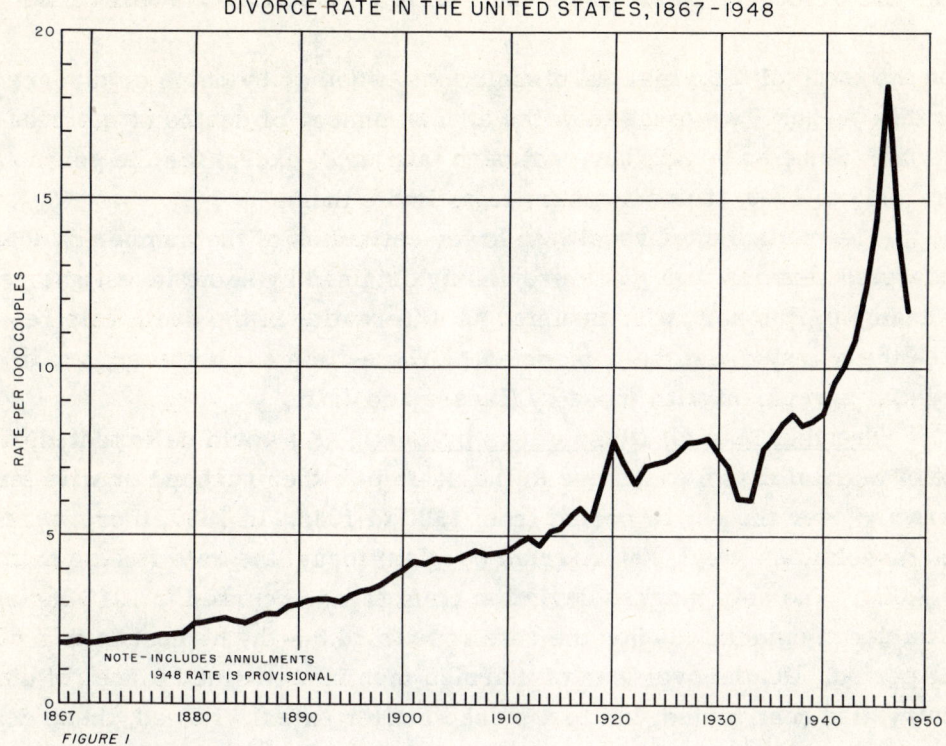

FIGURE 1

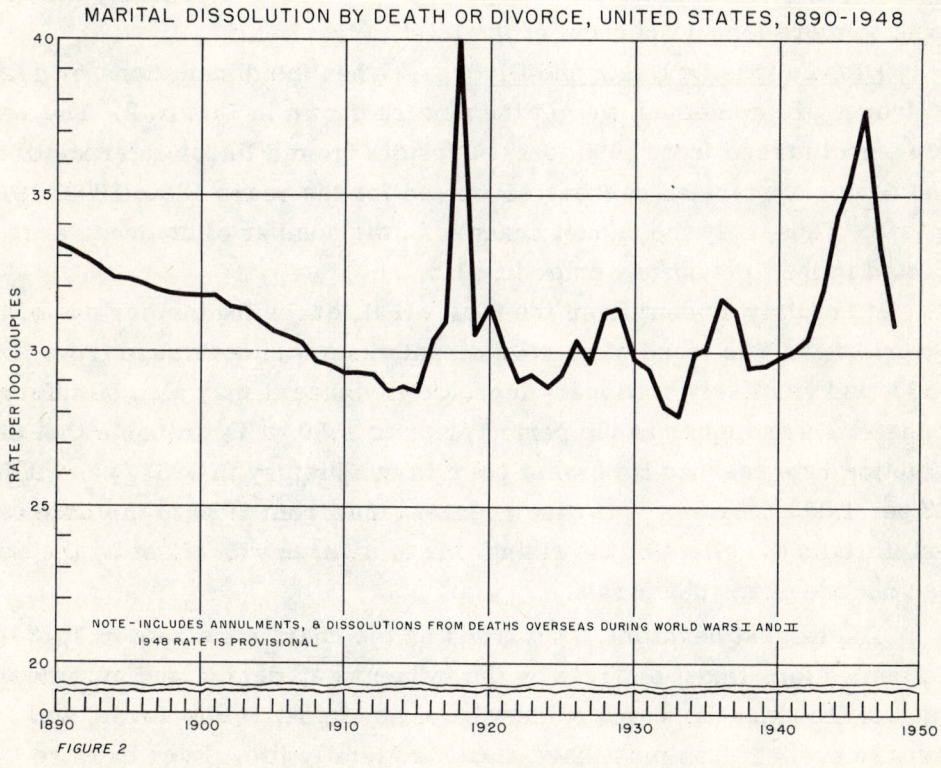

FIGURE 2

been the trend of total marital dissolutions, whether by death or divorce? For this purpose, we must know the annual number of deaths of married persons. Since such data have not been tabulated, except for the years from 1935 to 1940, it is necessary to estimate them.[5]

The method used results in lower estimates of the number of deaths of married persons than those previously obtained by some investigators, for example, Rubinow, who assumed no differential in the death rate between the married and the unmarried.[6] The estimates, however, are in essential agreement with those by Hauser and Jaffe.[7]

Trend of Marital Dissolutions by Death. As would be expected, the rate of marital dissolutions due to the death of either husband or wife tended downward over the entire period from 1890 to 1948. In 1890, there were 30 such dissolutions per 1,000 married couples; today, the rate is less than 20 per 1,000. The only marked deviation from trend occurred in 1918 during the influenza epidemic, when the rate rose to 34.6 — the highest in this 60-year period. Deaths overseas of married men in the armed forces of our country also contributed, but to a much smaller extent. Indeed, these deaths represented only about 4 percent of the total in 1918.[8] Deaths of American married men outside of continental United States during World War II were of greater magnitude, but even at their peak in 1944 they probably did not amount to more than 11 percent of the total in that year.[9]

Dissolutions by Death and Divorce. When the dissolutions by death and divorce are combined, we get the picture shown in Figure 2. The relatively smooth trend from 1890 to 1914 results from a linear interpolation of the deaths of married persons estimated for the years 1890, 1900, 1910, and 1915. Thus, only the annual changes in the number of divorces are reflected in the fluctuations prior to 1915.

It is fairly evident from the figure that, excluding the periods of the two world wars, the trend of marital dissolutions was downward from 1890 to 1915, and relatively stationary thereafter. Since it may also be inferred that the rate was higher in the period prior to 1890, it is probable that the dissolution rate reached its lowest point in our history in 1933, when it fell to 28 per 1,000 couples. It is also apparent that from 1920 to the time of Pearl Harbor, the effect of the rising tide of divorce was offset by the continued decline of the death rate.

The largest deviation from trend on the chart — the rate in 1918 — is accounted for almost entirely by the influenza epidemic, and provides an idea of the extent to which epidemics of smallpox, yellow fever, and cholera in earlier eras must have disrupted family life. Even in more recent years, prior to 1920, typhoid fever, tuberculosis, pneumonia, and the hazards of childbirth were the great homebreakers. Today, due to the outstanding advances in sanitation, medical science, and public health, these diseases have been virtually eliminated. At the same time, however, divorce has risen in importance. This is dramatically illustrated by the secondary peak on the chart—the period from 1944 to 1947, which is due primarily to the rise of the divorce rate during those years.

Relative Importance of Death and Divorce. The increasing importance of divorce in family dissolutions is clearly illustrated in Figure 3. Here, divorces are plotted as a percent of the total marital dissolutions. The proportion rises from 9 percent in 1890 to more than 20 percent by 1919, to somewhat above 30 percent by 1941, and to a little less than 50 percent in 1946—from which it has declined to 38 percent in 1948.[10]

This ratio was once thought to be a reliable index of the probability that a marriage would end in divorce. Actually, however, it overstates the chances of divorce, since new marriages are increasing, tending to over emphasize the number of divorces because the divorce rate is highest at the earlier durations of marriage (the more recent and larger marriage cohorts) whereas the death rate is highest at the later durations (the older and smaller cohorts).

Figure 4 illustrates the relationship between the divorce and death rates by duration of marriage for the first 40 years of marriage in 1947. Although 1947 is the latest year for which the divorce rate can be computed by duration of marriage, the general pattern would be similar regardless of which year was used.[11] However, the 1948 rates when available will undoubtedly be lower, especially at the earlier durations, which in 1947 were still greatly effected by the war.

According to the 1947 experience, the divorce rate reached its maximum in the third year of marriage when the rate was a little above 30 per 1,000, and thereafter it declined throughout the marital life span. In contrast, dissolutions due to mortality were at a minimum in the first five years of marriage.[12] Thereafter, however, the rate rose steadily with each advance in the number of years married. As a consequence, it is not until the 15th year of marriage (couples who have celebrated their 14th anniversary), that deaths exceed divorces as a cause of marital dissolutions.

The divorce and death rates combined give the total dissolution rate, which follows a modified form of a U-curve. The rate rises rapidly to a peak of almost 40 per 1,000 in the third year of marriage, declines

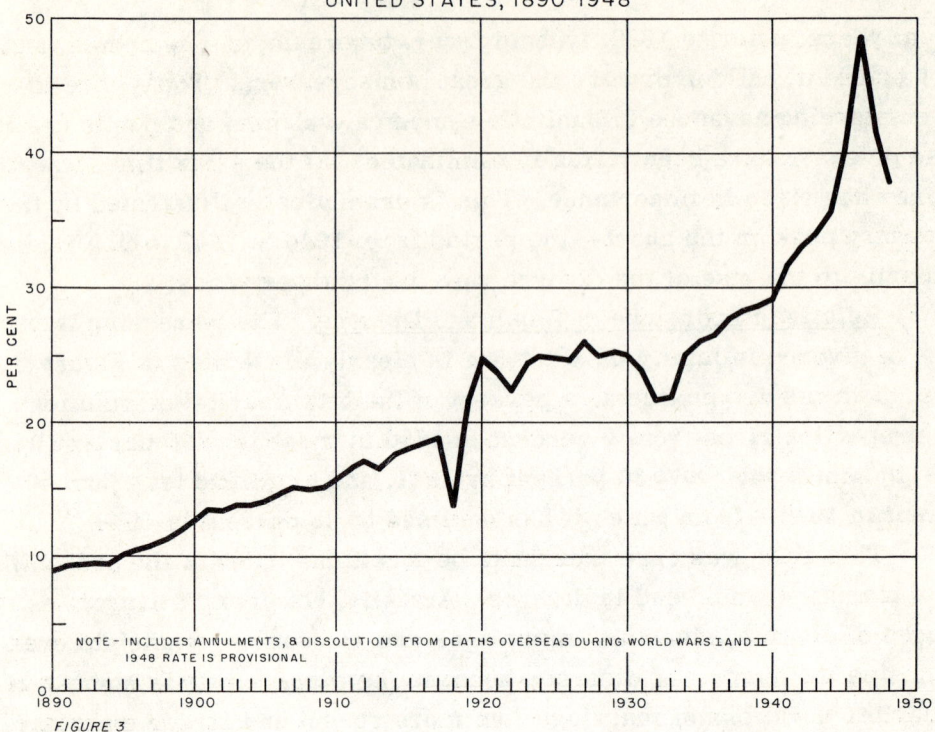

FIGURE 3

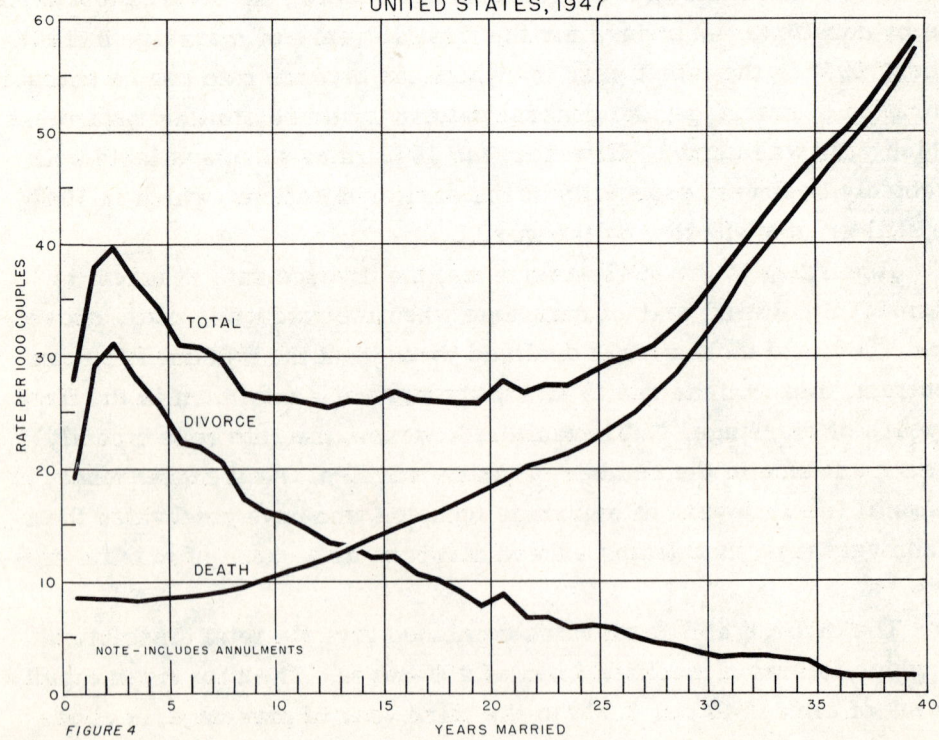

FIGURE 4

rapidly through the ninth year, after which it continues at about the level of 26 per 1,000 until the 20th year is reached. At the later durations, the rate increases steadily, virtually paralleling the rate due to deaths alone. However, it is not until the 32nd year of marriage that the dissolution rate at the longer durations exceeds the rate among newlyweds.

<u>Trend of Divorce Rates by Duration of Marriage</u>. Figure 5 shows the trend of the divorce rate by duration of marriage in five year marital-duration groups for the years from 1922 to 1947. This chart amply documents the fact that the recent upswing in the divorce rate was sharpest among those married less than five years — essentially those married during the war. Thus, from 1941 to 1946, the probability of divorce or annulment within the first five years of marriage more than doubled. Smaller but still appreciable increases also occurred among families of longer standing, but the relative rise was progressively smaller for each successive five years of marriage. However, even among those married twenty years or longer, the rate in 1946 was one-third higher than in 1941. Although the rates declined sharply from 1946 to 1947, the 1947 rates were still among the highest in our history.

Another point of interest disclosed by the figure is the pattern of the decline of the divorce rate during the depression of the 1930's. These estimates indicate a change opposite to that of the recent war period. Early in the depression decade the divorce rate appears to have declined the most among couples married only a relatively short time, and the decline to have persisted for one year longer among them than for those married longer.

Viewing the 1922-1947 period as a whole, an upward trend is evident for each marital-duration group. Indeed, if the 1947 rates persisted, more than one out of every three marriages in our country would eventually be dissolved by divorce. However, the rate declined sharply in 1948 and probably will decline further in the near future. This does not mean that the long-term upward trend has been reversed; rather, the decline probably is a temporary phenomenon which has followed each postwar peak.

Since the frequency of divorce is subject to marked changes from year to year, especially in periods of major stress and strain such as occur during depressions and wars, it is misleading to gauge the rate of marital dissolution by the divorce rate recorded in a particular year. How then can we secure a reasonably accurate index of the extent to which marriages are being terminated by divorce? The next figure throws some light on this problem.

Figure 6 shows the divorce rates in the first 25 years of marriage—

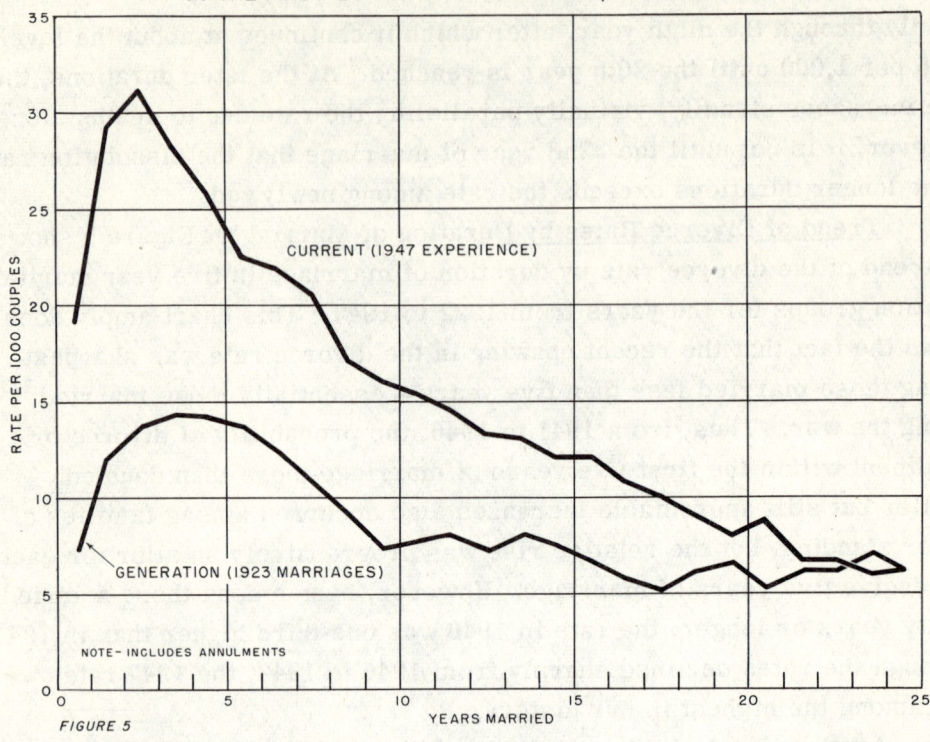

FIGURE 5. Comparison of generation and current divorce rates in the first 25 years of marriage, United States.

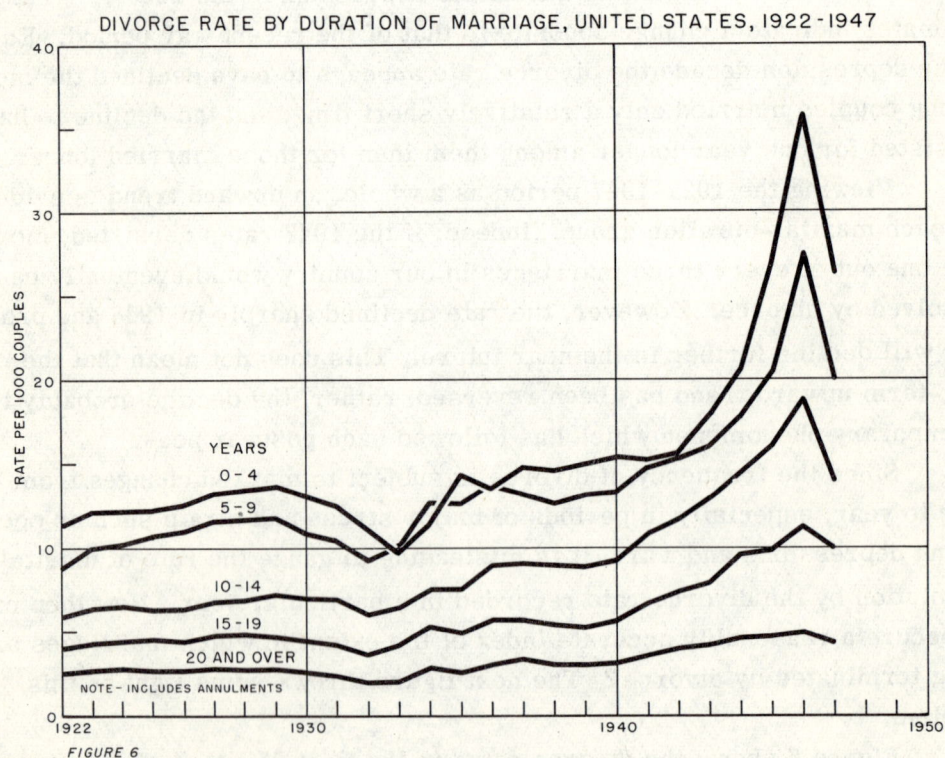

FIGURE 6. Divorce rate by duration of marriage, United States, 1922-1947.

MARITAL DISSOLUTIONS IN THE UNITED STATES

those recorded in 1947 compared with the rates actually experienced by couples married in 1923. The current rates are decidedly higher than those experienced by the 1923 cohort. Indeed, in contrast to the figure of more than one out of every three marriages ending in divorce, which is indicated by the 1947 rates, probably fewer than one out of every four marriages begun in 1923 will eventually be dissolved by divorce. Since the divorce rate in each group of marriages of specified duration has moved upward since 1923, it is evident that the proportion of marriages ending in divorce for couples married in recent years will exceed the figure for the 1923 cohort, but not to the extent indicated by the divorce rates for the war and early postwar period. For example, only 11 percent of the marriages contracted in 1923 were dissolved by divorce within ten years, compared with 16 percent for those begun in 1938. According to the rates recorded in 1947, as many as 21 percent would end in divorce or annulment within the first ten years of marriage.

Although it is not possible to predict the future trend of the divorce rate in the present state of our knowledge of social, economic, and psychological factors, it would not be surprising if the divorce rate resumes its historic upward trend in the 1950's, though perhaps at a lesser rate of increase than in the past. If this should occur, it is likely that the divorce rate experienced in future years by couples married ten years or more would be fairly similar to the 1947 rate for comparable groups. Under these circumstances, more than one-fourth but less than one-third of the marriages contracted in the prewar years will eventually be ended by divorce or annulment. Thus, for example, it is probable that about 30 percent of the 1938 marriages will ultimately be dissolved by divorce.

APPLICATION OF DEMOGRAPHIC DATA TO CURRENT PROBLEMS

Appendix Note 1

Method Used to Estimate the Number of Deaths of Married Persons. The ratio of the death rate for the married to the death rate for all persons was computed by age and sex groups for 1900, 1924-1928, and 1940.[13] Values of the ratios for 1910, 1915 to 1920, 1929 to 1934 were obtained by interpolation; the ratios for 1900 were used for 1890. For the years prior to 1935, these ratios were multiplied by the death rates for the death registration states to obtain the estimated death rates for married persons in the United States. The latter, in turn, were multiplied by the estimated married population to secure the number of deaths of married persons. By this means, the number of deaths was estimated for a series of key years (1890, 1900, 1910, 1915 to 1920, 1924 to 1934). The deaths for these key years were then interpolated to derive the estimates for the intervening years (1891, 1892, etc.). For the years 1941 to 1947, the number of deaths of married persons in the United States was estimated on the assumption that the ratios in mortality among the marital classes at each age and sex remained the same as in 1940.[14] The sum of the deaths of all marital classes was then adjusted to the recorded total in each age-sex group, by pro-rating the differences between the computed and actual totals. The 1948 estimates are provisional.

In view of the sharp rise in the death rate during the influenza epidemic, it is of interest to note that the annual changes in the estimated number of deaths for married persons in the United States from 1916 to 1920 closely parallels those recorded in New York State.

Deaths Among Married Persons, 1916-1920; 1916 = 100

Year	New York State (Recorded)	United States (Estimated)
1916	100.0	100.0
1917	104.6	104.4
1918	140.3	141.1
1919	101.6	101.6
1920	100.7	102.8

Appendix Note 2

Method Used to Compute Duration-Specific Divorce Rates. With divorces and annulments granted in any calendar year distributed by their duration of marriage, it was necessary to have the distribution by duration of marriage of all married couples, in order to compute the duration-specific rates. For this purpose, cohorts entering 0-duration in any specified calendar year were estimated as the average of the number of marriages performed in the preceding and specified calendar year. The cohorts were then traced forward in time by subtracting the number dissolved by death, divorce, and annulment in each subsequent year. The method is a variant of those used by Cahen and Monahan.

To obtain the number of couples at durations after the 40th year of marriage, which is needed to compute the proportion of marriages eventually ending in divorce, the "cohort" data were projected to the later durations on the basis of Census data showing the duration of present marital status for married females in April 1948.[15]

Representativeness of the Data Used to Distribute Divorces and Annulments by Duration of Marriage. For the years from 1922 to 1932, data on divorces and annulments by duration of marriage are available in the reports on marriage and divorce published by the Bureau of the Census. For the later years these data had to be estimated from statistics supplied by Cleveland, Ohio (Cuyahoga County) and 14 States (Alabama, Florida, Iowa, Michigan, Mississippi, Montana, New Hampshire, Oregon, Rhode Island, South Dakota, Tennessee, Virginia, Wisconsin, Wyoming). Unfortunately, the data could not be obtained from each of these States for each of the calendar years involved, so that the information available by duration of marriage varied from as little as 5.5 percent of the nationwide total in 1933 to 15.9 percent in 1944. However, the different "collection areas" used for each of the years from 1933 to 1947 do give an unbiased estimate of the duration of marriages ended by divorce or annulment in 1931. (Also, see footnote 15).

APPLICATION OF DEMOGRAPHIC DATA TO CURRENT PROBLEMS

FOOTNOTES

1. This paper is the second in a series based on research for a doctoral dissertation in the Department of Sociology, Columbia University. All 1948 data are provisional. Acknowledgment is made to Mr. Mortimer Spiegelman, Assistant Statistician of the Metropolitan Life Insurance Company, for helpful suggestions and technical advice.

2. The number of married couples in the United States for 1867-1889 was taken from Walter F. Willcox: Studies in American Demography, Cornell University Press, 1940, page 344; those for 1890-1948 were computed from data on marriages performed, estimates of the number of deaths of married persons (see Appendix Note 1), number of married males reported in the Censuses of 1890 to 1940, and number of married females estimated from Census surveys in 1944 and 1946-1948.

3. Walter F. Willcox: The Divorce Problem, Doctoral Dissertation, Faculty of Political Science, Columbia University, 1891, page 16.

4. Ibid, page 19. See also, Introduction to the Vital Statistics of the United States, 1900 to 1930, Bureau of the Census, Washington, 1933, pages 50-51, and 124; and Studies in American Demography, pages 348-349.

5. See Appendix Note 1.

6. I. M. Rubinow: Some Statistical Aspects of Marriage and Divorce, Pamphlet Series No. 3, The American Academy of Political and Social Science, Philadelphia, 1936, Deaths of Married Persons from 1910 to 1930, pages 16-19.

7. P. M. Hauser and A. J. Jaffe: "The Extent of the Housing Shortage," Law and Contemporary Problems, XII (i):3-15, Winter, 1947. This paper contains estimates of the number of families broken by death, 1930-1945. The estimates for 1939-1943 and 1945 appear to be somewhat too high. For example, the 1940 estimate includes the deaths of divorced persons and of all persons of unknown marital status.

8. It is estimated that 31,780 married men died overseas during World War I, of whom 29,480 died in 1918.

9. It is estimated that 167,340 American married men died outside of continental United States during World War II, of whom 80,400 died in 1944 and 52,680 in 1945. The figures include an allowance for deaths of merchant seamen.

10. Compare with Alfred Cahen: Statistical Analysis of American Divorce, Columbia University Press, 1932, pages 30-31; I. M. Rubinow: Some Statistical Aspects of Marriage and Divorce, page 20; and Walter F. Willcox: Studies in American Demography, page 348.

11. The divorces and annulments granted in the United States in 1947 were classified by duration of marriage according to their distribution in ten States (Florida, Iowa, Mississippi, Montana, New Hampshire, Rhode Island, South Dakota, Tennessee, Virginia, and Wyoming) and the City of Cleveland, Ohio. For explanation of the method used to compute the duration-specific rates and a note on the representativeness of the data for the situation in the country as a whole, see Appendix Note 2.

12. The dissolution rate from mortality was computed by duration of marriage on the basis of the age-sex-specific death rates for married persons in 1940, weighted according to the age distribution of husbands and wives in

MARITAL DISSOLUTIONS IN THE UNITED STATES

each duration of marriage. The latter was estimated from data on duration of the present marital status by age and sex for married persons in the United States in April 1948 (Current Population Reports, P-20, No. 23, Bureau of the Census, Washington, March 4, 1949, pages 12 and 13). This method results in much higher mortality dissolution rates than the methods previously used by Alfred Cahen (previous citation) and Thomas P. Monahan ("The Changing Probability of Divorce," American Sociological Review, Vol. V, No. 4, August 1940, page 538). Unfortunately, some variant of the method used by Cahen or Monahan is the only one which can be used for the earlier years. Then, too, it should be noted that there is some advantage in the use of "low" death rates for the years prior to World War I and for the early 1920's, since the number of married couples in the population was increased by net migration to the United States during those years. In contrast, it would appear desirable to use "high" death rates for the years from 1925 to 1940, since the increase in the number of married couples reported in the decennial censuses for that period is smaller than the number expected from the addition of new marriages and the subtraction of marriages ended by death and divorce.

13. The death rates by marital status for 1900 were computed from data in the reports of the 12th Census, Washington, 1902 — Vol. III, Vital Statistics, Part I, Analysis and Ratio Tables, page 14, for deaths in the death registration states of 1900; and Vol. II, Population, Part II, table 30, for the population in each of the death registration states. Those for 1924-1928 are based on data published by Walter F. Willcox: Introduction to the Vital Statistics of the United States, page 109; and for 1940, on deaths in Vital Statistics, Special Reports, Vol. 23, No. 7, Bureau of the Census, Washington, 1945, page 137 (with deaths of unknown age and marital status distributed) and on population in Population, Vol. IV, Part I, 16th Census, Bureau of the Census, Washington, 1943.

14. Mortimer Spiegelman: "Mortality in Relation to Widowhood," Proceedings of the American Philosophical Society, Vol. 80, No. 4, 1939, page 548.

15. The Bureau's data for April 1948 provide a crude measure of the accuracy of the method used to estimate the distribution of married couples by duration of marriage. The following table compares the Census data for married females with the data obtained by the method described in Appendix Note 2.

Number of Married Couples (Thousands)

Number of Years Married	Bureau of the Census April 1948	Estimated January 1, 1948
0	1,280	1,708 (prov.)
1	1,559	2,083
2-4	4,449	4,472
5-9	6,513	6,344
10-14	5,030	4,897
15-19	3,749 (approx.)	3,714
20-29	6,683 (approx.)	6,883
30-39	4,294 (est.)	4,367

The data are fairly similar except for the first two years of marriage. Considering the fact that the annual number of marriages performed in the years ended April 1947 and April 1948 was close to two million, it is likely that the Census data understate the number of couples married for less than two years.

TOTAL MARITAL DISSOLUTIONS IN THE UNITED STATES, RELATIVE IMPORTANCE OF MORTALITY AND DIVORCE: DISCUSSION

Samuel C. Newman
National Office of Vital Statistics

Everyone working with United States marriage and divorce data realizes they are inadequate, and will welcome this effort by Mr. Jacobson to construct the patterns of recent trends with whatever fragmentary materials are at hand. His comments on the limitations of the data should be borne in mind, for it has been necessary to make estimates based on estimates. Besides the rough substantiations presented of some of the estimates, we may mention a study by Hauser and Jaffe on "The Extent of the Housing Shortage" (Law and Contemporary Problems, Vol. XII, No. 1) in which they estimated the number of families broken by death and divorce.

The current program of the National Office of Vital Statistics, in the Public Health Service of the Federal Security Agency, with respect to marriage and divorce data is limited to numbers of occurrences (in some cases, estimates only), with no detailed statistics such as those needed for the analysis of the present topic. It is encouraging that the states in increasing number have provided for integration of their marriage and divorce records and statistics with their other vital records and vital statistics. The national office hopes to compile detailed statistics from as many of the state offices as can furnish them. But more adequate vital statistics of marriages and divorces would not answer all questions in this area. Much can be gained from census-type population data on marital status, the family, etc. These two types of data are complementary, and both need more development.

As the paper points out, the gap in data for the recent war and postwar period cannot be remedied by more adequate data for future years. Mr. Jacobson's study is a valuable contribution toward filling this gap.

THE LENGTH OF WORKING LIFE
Summary[1]

Seymour L. Wolfbein
Bureau of Labor Statistics

In common with the conventional life table, the table of working life considers an initial group of 100,000 persons at birth and follows it through life, subject to a pattern of attrition determined by a specified set of mortality rates. Beginning at age 14, the life-table population is exposed to the probabilities of accession and of separation from the labor force at different ages. Age-specific rates of labor force participation were developed from census data for April, 1940. Net rates of accession and separation from the labor force were then derived from the differences in successive worker rates. In dividing separations into those due to death and those due to "retirement," which includes all causes other than death, it was necessary, for lack of differential mortality rates for members and non-members of the labor force, to assume that age-specific death rates for men in the labor force approximated those for the general population. In 1940, the average male worker age 20 had a life expectancy of 46.8 additional years and a labor force life expectancy of 41.1 years. Thus he could look forward to an average of almost 6 years of life in retirement. In recent decades there has been a constant tendency for working-life expectancy to lag behind the extension of the life span, although between 1940 and 1947 this trend halted, at least temporarily. Rural labor force life is, in general, longer than urban, starting sooner and ending later. At age 20 the labor-life expectancy for nonwhites is less than that for whites because of the higher mortality rates for nonwhites between the ages of 20 and 50. The method used in estimating the future working-life span in this paper is only one of several alternatives. For example, the average number of remaining years of labor force participation could have been calculated by relating total remaining labor force participation to the total number of persons living rather than to persons in the labor force.

APPLICATION OF DEMOGRAPHIC DATA TO CURRENT PROBLEMS

FOOTNOTE

1. This summary was prepared by the editor, and is taken from the report of the annual meeting, <u>Population Index</u>, Vol. 15, No. 3 (July, 1949). The paper is to appear in full in <u>Population Studies</u>, Dec., 1949, Vol. 3, No. 3.

THE LENGTH OF WORKING LIFE: DISCUSSION

A. J. Jaffe
U. S. Bureau of the Census

Within the scope of a brief discussion it is obviously impossible to present a detailed critical evaluation of the methodology and problems inherent in calculating working force life tables. However, having examined in detail Dr. Wolfbein's work on this subject I do not hesitate to say that, in my opinion, this is a sound methodological study.

One question raised by Dr. Wolfbein was with respect to whether the probabilities used in constructing working force life tables should be based on the total population, or limited to the population in the working force. In this connection it would appear that there is no uniquely correct way for calculating probabilities; rather, there are many ways of making such calculations, each of which is correct, and each of which has its own specific meaning. Accordingly, in trying to decide the nature of the probability to be calculated it is first necessary to determine the nature of the problem for which an answer is desired. Since there are a large number of problems and questions which can be raised there probably are a large number of different ways in which working force life tables can be calculated, each of which is correct within the limits set by the question as originally posed. Incidentally, this problem is not unique to working force life tables but is common to all probability tables. Unfortunately, this discussant knows of no comprehensive and thorough study which has attempted to structuralize the entire subject of probability tables.

It is clear that this device has great potential research use, both for practical and theoretical purposes. One direction which should be taken, is that of calculating working force life tables for separate occupational groups. Either individual occupations or groups of allied occupations ought to be separately studied, and the requisite tables calculated. As soon as such work is attempted, however, we are faced with the fact that mortality data for occupational groups are not available because so far, the many and varied problems inherent in the accurate reporting of occupations have

APPLICATION OF DEMOGRAPHIC DATA TO CURRENT PROBLEMS

not been solved. It is quite clear, therefore, that if any significant degree of further progress is to be made in the utilization of the working force life table technique, serious attempts will have to be made again to obtain useable occupational mortality data.

Finally, it seems pertinent to point out that the average number of years of retirement—that is the difference between the average age at death and the average age of leaving the working force—may turn out to be a highly valuable social and cultural index. Comparison of such figures among a number of countries and for various time periods may reveal highly significant economic, technological and cultural differences. As nations develop economically and technologically and machine power replaces human muscles, opportunities for leisure and retirement, as well as a higher plane-of-living and its attendant demographic and social phenomena, also develop. Such changes in the methods of work and in the economic and social environment should be mirrored in the average number of years of retirement. What little work has been done to date in the United States suggests the usefulness of such a figure and points to the desirability of further investigation.

REPORT ON A SERIES OF ILLEGAL ABORTIONS INDUCED BY PHYSICIANS*

Christopher Tietze, M.D.
National Committee on Maternal Health

Several investigators[1,2,4,5,7] have presented evidence to show that at least in urban areas of the United States the great majority of illegal abortions are induced by physicians. These cases are rarely admitted to hospitals for completion or for the treatment of complications and they do not often appear in studies of mortality. Little is known about them except that they are very numerous.

Through good fortune the author has come into possession of a series of 363 records representing the practice of two such abortion specialists in a large Eastern city during several months in 1948. Thanks are due to the individuals who have made this material accessible for research. The reader must be satisfied with the author's assurance that the records are genuine, complete, and probably as good as those kept by most practitioners and clinics. However, the material does not lend itself to a study of the course of recovery or of sequelae.

All but one of these abortions were performed between the 5th and 13th weeks of pregnancy, counting from the estimated date of conception. The average period of gestation was 8.5 weeks. One pregnancy was interrupted in the 15th week. It is not known why this particular patient was accepted at that advanced stage.

The records do not contain usable information concerning the occupational, social, or economic background of the clientele. It is known, however, that the fees charged varied from $300 to $500, which should indicate a fairly high level of income. Of the 363 women, 102 were single, 180 or 49.6 ± 2.6 percent married, and 81 previously married. About half of the latter group were widows, the others divorced. The percentage of married women was lower than but not significantly different from that reported by Hamilton[3] in New York and much lower than among the cases studied by Simons[6] in Minneapolis who found three-fourths of the induced cases in the married group. Since his were hospital patients their abortions had been induced either by the pregnant woman herself or by a midwife or other non-medical abortionist. Many were probably drawn from the underprivileged group where economic pressure on the married woman is comparatively greater and social pressure on the unmarried woman perhaps less than in the class from which the present series is recruited. Another factor contributing to the difference may be a greater willingness on the part of married women to seek admission to a hospital for the treatment of abortion, whereas the unmarried will tend to avoid hospitalization unless it is clearly necessary because of fever or other complications.

The women in the present series ranged in age from 13 to 47 years (Table I). The average age was 28.6 years. As one would expect the single women were youngest; while for the married and the previously married the average age was practically the same.

Of the group as a whole 170 or almost half had never borne a child (Table I). The childless included all but two of the single women, one-fourth of the married, and one-third of the previously married. The total number of children born was 397 for the whole group, including 303 reported by the married women. The average number of children ever born was 1.09 for the group as a whole and 1.68 for the married.

It is of interest to compare the married women in this series with a group of women delivered on the private service of a large hospital in the same city in 1948. Table II presents a comparison in terms of children born before the current abortion or delivery. The differences are striking. They confirm earlier findings[1,4,8,9] that the incidence of illegal induced abortion tends to increase with parity and suggest that in this group abortion was used primarily not as a method of child spacing but of limiting the ultimate size of the family. This was probably not true for the ten married women, 15-19 years old, in the abortion series. There was only one case in this age group among the 481 deliveries. This seems to indicate that illegal abortions are also resorted to by those who are not yet ready to shoulder the responsibilities of raising a family.

In addition to their 397 children the women in this series reported 29 unintentional abortions. This number represents seven percent of all pregnancies terminating without interference. This is a plausible ratio which is only slightly lower than one would expect on the basis of earlier studies.[5,10] It adds to the general credibility of the records.

Sixty-five women, or 17.9 percent of the group, admitted one or more induced abortions preceding the current one (Table I). The proportion was not significantly different for the single, the married, and the

ILLEGAL ABORTIONS INDUCED BY PHYSICIANS

previously married. This information is probably more complete than it is likely to be in a series of different origin because there was apparently less reason for dissimulation. The total number of previous induced abortions was 101, representing one-fifth of all previous pregnancies. Many of them had been performed by the same operators as the current one.

If the proposition is accepted that first and later induced abortions had an equal chance of being represented in our sample, then the average number of induced abortions in the population from which this sample is drawn can be estimated to be on the order of 1.2 (363/298) per woman. This figure, of course, refers only to those women who had at least one induced abortion during their reproductive lives. Since many women never resort to illegal abortion the average number for all women must have been much lower, but it cannot be computed from this series of records.

As far as the author is aware this is the first series of illegal abortions induced by physicians ever reported on in American medical literature. The number of cases is not large and it cannot be estimated how far the findings are typical of the activities of abortion specialists around the country. Much work remains to be done until we shall have adequate knowledge of this much neglected field of human behavior.

APPLICATION OF DEMOGRAPHIC DATA TO CURRENT PROBLEMS

TABLE I

Women Undergoing Illegal Abortion by Marital Status, Age, Number of Children Ever Born, and Previous Induced Abortions

Age (Years)	Single	Married	Previously Married	Total
10 - 14	3	-	-	3
15 - 19	22	10	2	34
20 - 24	29	44	15	88
25 - 29	21	42	28	91
30 - 34	18	42	20	80
35 - 39	6	19	10	35
40 and over	3	23	6	32
Children Born				
0	100	45	25	170
1	2	39	31	72
2	-	52	16	68
3	-	27	8	35
4 and over	-	17	1	18
Previous Abortions				
0	87	147	64	298
1	10	18	15	43
2	2	10	2	14
3 and over	3	5	-	8
Total	102	180	81	363

TABLE II

Comparison of 180 Married Women Undergoing Illegal Abortions and 481 Women Delivered on Private Service in 1948

Previous Children	Number of Cases		Percent Distribution		Ratio of Percentages
	Abortions	Deliveries	Abortions	Deliveries	
0	45	206	25.0	42.8	3 : 5
1	39	164	21.7	34.1	2 : 3
2	52	86	28.9	17.9	5 : 3
3	27	21	15.0	4.4	3 : 1
4 and over	17	4	9.4	.8	11 : 1
Total	180	481	100.0	100.0	-

ILLEGAL ABORTIONS INDUCED BY PHYSICIANS

FOOTNOTES

* Reprinted from Human Biology. 21 (1): pp. 60-64. February, 1949.

1. Brunner, E.K. "The Outcome of 1556 Conceptions." Human Biology. 13 (2): 159-176. 1941.

2. Brunner, E.K. and Newton, L. "Abortions in Relation to Viable Births in 10,609 Pregnancies." Am. J. Obst. and Gyn. 38 (1): 82-90. 1939.

3. Hamilton, V.C. "Some Sociologic and Psychologic Observations on Abortion." Am. J. Obst. and Gyn. 39 (6): 919-928. 1940.

4. Kopp, M. Birth Control in Practice. New York, 1934.

5. National Committee on Maternal Health. The Abortion Problem. Baltimore, 1944.

6. Simons, J.H. "Statistical Analysis of One Thousand Abortions." Am. J. Obst. and Gyn. 37 (5): 840-849. 1939.

7. Stix, R.K. "A Study of Pregnancy Wastage." Milbank Memorial Fund Quarterly. 13 (4): 347-365. 1935.

8. Stix, R.K. and Notestein, F.W. Controlled Fertility. Baltimore, 1940.

9. Whelpton, P.K. and Kiser, C.V. "The Comparative Influence on Fertility of Contraception and Impairments of Fecundity." Milbank Memorial Fund Quarterly. 26 (2): 303-357. 1948.

10. Wiehl, D.G. "A Summary of Data on Reported Incidence of Abortion." Milbank Memorial Fund Quarterly. 16 (1): 1-9. 1938.

SECTION II

TOOLS FOR DEMOGRAPHIC RESEARCH

Morning Session, May 29, 1949
Philip M. Hauser, University of Chicago, Chairman

OUR CURRENT DEMOGRAPHIC INVENTORY:
REVIEW OF DATA FROM THE CURRENT POPULATION SURVEY
Summary[1]

A. Ross Eckler
U. S. Bureau of the Census

The Current Population Survey of the Bureau of the Census is essentially a minature census of the United States taken once a month on the basis of interviews with about 25,000 households. The households are located in 68 counties or groups of 2 or 3 counties which have been scientifically selected from strata set up in accordance with such factors as geographical location, industrial or agricultural characteristics, proportion of nonwhite population, proportion in rural areas, etc. Within the 68 areas, sample households are selected in accordance with the principles of probability sampling. This is insured through the predesignation of specified small areas within which the canvassers list all dwelling units and systematically select certain ones for interview.

The families included in the survey are interviewed over a period of 6 successive months, after which they are replaced by other families in the interest of public relations. In order to reduce the impact upon the results of changing to a new group of families, the shifts are spread as uniformly as possible during the year. Since the amount of turnover from one month to the next is limited to 20-percent, 80-percent of the families are identical for any consecutive pair of months.

The Current Population Survey is the product of extensive work in the Research Division of the Work Projects Administration in the late '30's which led to a plan for the direct measurement of the volume of unemployment through canvassing a sample of the population in order to determine the work status of each individual. By this means it was possible for the first time to get a direct measure of the number of people seeking work, whereas previous estimates of unemployment had been obtained by the indirect procedure of subtracting the number of unemployed from a projected labor force total.

TOOLS FOR DEMOGRAPHIC RESEARCH

By early 1942 the need for the series as a measure of unemployment had decreased sharply, and accordingly consideration was given to the desirability of transferring the organization from the Work Projects Administration to some permanent agency. After careful consideration of several possible transfers, the Budget Bureau shifted the operation to the Bureau of the Census because of the close relationship of the work to the demographic program of the Bureau of the Census and because of the possibilities afforded for the development of a generalized statistical collection service for other Federal agencies.

The present procedures for the Current Population Survey, which have been essentially unchanged for the past several years involve, as already noted, a rigorously prescribed procedure for selecting sample households. For each family brought into the sample a control card is filled out at the beginning of the six-month series of interviews which lists the names of all members of the family, their ages, and a few other facts. Then, for each of the monthly interviews that follow a standard series of recurring questions is asked to establish the facts of employment and unemployment, as well as certain supplemental questions on a variety of demographic subjects.

There are a number of methods by which the basic operations represented by the current population survey program have been modified to provide substantial amounts of demographic data in addition to those regularly furnished. It is possible to expand a sample in a variety of ways so as to give additional information. In April 1947, for example, the national sample was substantially increased so that regional figures could be provided for a number of important population characteristics. In that same month, the number of households interviewed in some of the large cities in the monthly sample were substantially expanded and samples were taken in a number of additional cities, providing thereby population, labor force, and housing data for 34 metropolitan districts. At the present time (May, 1949) a similar sample is being canvassed in the city of Chicago and the surrounding territory to provide current data on a number of subjects important to that area. It should be noted also that the month-to-month linkage provided by the 80-percent of the sample which is always interviewed in two successive months makes possible a study of the dynamics of the labor force and other demographic subjects which could not be measured in any other way.

The usefulness of the Current Population Survey as a source of current demographic information is perhaps best indicated by comparison

REVIEW OF DATA FROM THE CURRENT POPULATION SURVEY

of the types of current information available in the last five years and those available in the corresponding period a decade ago. In the last half of the 1930's, the releases on population subjects were limited to presenting population projections or giving figures on children under institutional care and in foster homes. By contrast, the table below shows the very considerable number of releases on various subjects which have been made possible through the Current Population Survey.

Number of releases: 1944 to May 1949

Subject	National	Regional	Metropolitan Districts
Population by residence	14	1	
Marital status and families	12	2	34
Education and school attendance	10	1	34
Migration	9	1	34
Income	4		
Fertility	1	1	
Housing	6	1	34

In addition to the releases counted in the table above, there have been monthly releases on employment and unemployment since 1940, some 20 special releases on labor force subjects for the country as a whole, and data on the number of employed and unemployed for some 50 cities and metropolitan districts. A listing of the specific releases referred to in the table can be obtained from the current catalog of the Census Bureau, or by written request to the Bureau.

It is outside the scope of this brief statement to undertake to describe the demographic information which has been made available through the Current Population Survey. However, the wide range of the subjects covered is indicated by the fact that the survey has provided evidence on the amount of doubling up of families, the participation of married women in the labor force, the characteristics of women who have contributed to the recent rise in the birth rate, changes in school attendance patterns, the relationship between highest grade completed and literacy, the nature of moves and reasons for moving, the number of marginal and part-time workers, and the changes in housing facilities since 1940.

FOOTNOTE

1. This summary was prepared for publication by the author, A. Ross Eckler.

RECENT PROPOSALS FOR MODIFYING THE NET REPRODUCTION RATE
Summary[1]

T. J. Woofter, Jr.
Federal Security Agency

Three general uses to which the net reproduction rate has been put are to be distinguished: first, study of two or more populations in a given year or one population over time; second, analysis of factors affecting fertility; and third, prediction of the future. Especially in the last case confusion has resulted from careless use of the net reproduction rate by those not familiar with all of its assumptions. The principal objections that have been raised against the net reproduction rate are that it applies only to females, thus omitting from consideration the sex ratio and the relative ages of the parents; that it assumes the continuance of the reproductive patterns of a given instant; and that it ignores the influence of past experience upon the current fertility of women. The several proposals for modifying the net reproduction rate include male reproduction rates, which are analagous to the usual female rates and may be used together with the latter to get a measure of the effect of the sex ratio and of differences in age-specific nuptiality and mortality rates for males and females; nuptial reproduction rates of two types, those based on births of a single year standardized for duration of marriage, and those involving the number of children ever born to women married for varying lengths of time; generation rates, based on the total number of children born to a group of women who have completed the childbearing period; standardized quota reproduction rates, a new proposal to preserve the generation principle but with the experience centered closer to the current year; and finally, rates adjusted for birth order of children, either current year data or generation data being used. The rates summarized above fall into two general groups, those based on the experience of a single calendar year and perhaps subject to violent fluctuations, and those using the experience of the same group of women as they pass through life. The latter rates provide a less accurate representation of the immediate present but are more stable and take

RECENT PROPOSALS FOR MODIFYING THE NET REPRODUCTION RATE

into account the effects of past experience. It may be impossible to develop a single measure that will reflect the condition of the moment and at the same time provide a basis for the measurement of underlying trends.

FOOTNOTE

1. This summary was prepared by the editor, and is taken from the report of the annual meeting, Population Index, Vol. 15, No. 3 (July, 1949). The paper is to appear in full in the Journal of the American Statistical Association, Dec., 1949, Vol. 44, No. 248.

RECENT PROPOSALS FOR MODIFYING
THE NET REPRODUCTION RATE: DISCUSSION[1]

John Hajnal
Population Division, United Nations

Dr. Woofter, at the end of his paper, makes a distinction between two types of measures of reproductivity— "Those which use as their basis the experience of a single calendar year" and those which "follow the generation technique." I think that the introduction of measures of the generation type represents a most important development in recent work, but that this development is only incidentally connected with the problem of reproduction rates. Increasing attention is being paid to a new type of measure which can be widely applied in many fields. Dr. Woofter refers to a measure of the generation type which is not in the form of a reproduction rate, namely "the cumulated number of children born to women who were married at a certain time." Another example of the kind of statistic I have in mind is the proportion of persons in an age group who are or have been married. Such measures show what might be called the "stock" of certain events, such as births or first marriages, accumulated before a certain time by cohorts of persons starting the experience of life or marriage together. By contrast, all the usual marriage and fertility rates measure the "flow," i.e. the rate at which additions to the "stock" occur. Until recently, measures of the "stock" type have been rarely used, and the distinction between the two types has not been appreciated. Sometimes the two have been confused, as when proportions married are referred to as marriage rates.

Measures of the "stock" type are particularly important for investigating the recent recovery of the birth rate, which as Dr. Woofter points out, has powerfully stimulated recent development in the technique of analysis. For example, facts such as that in Great Britain, marriages contracted in 1927 had had by 1937 about as many children as the marriages contracted in 1937 had by 1947, cannot be deduced from the fluctuations of fertility which measure the "flow." The interest of such a statement is not primarily connected with the possibility of using "stock" data for the com-

MODIFYING THE NET REPRODUCTION RATE: DISCUSSION

putation of reproduction rates. The investigations of Whelpton on the children born to sucessive cohorts of women in the United States illustrate the same point. It does not matter whether all births or only female births are counted. Births of particular parity or occurring before the cohort has reached a particular age may also be considered separately. Such data bear no resemblance to reproduction rates.

A second line of development in recent work in fertility is aimed specifically at producing novel indices in the form of reproduction rates. Dr. Woofter lists several such attempts. In very rough terms, it may be said that such rates indicate how many births a generation of persons would produce throughout their lifetime under certain specified conditions. In speaking of "persons," I am ignoring the complications arising out of the distinction between paternal and maternal reproduction rates. For the sake of simplicity, I shall not try to be fully precise in some other respects. I think the essential characteristic of reproduction rates may be brought out be describing their computation in the following terms. On the basis of frequencies (of marriage, births, deaths) observed in a population, a series of rates is constructed which show the number of births which would be produced at each age by a cohort of persons subjected throughout their life to the frequencies in question. The rates showing the number of births at each age are then added up. I shall call any sum of such rates a reproduction rate. The conventional net reproduction rate is only one special computation of this sort.

What purposes are served by reproduction rates? Computation of a reproduction rate is mainly a technique for determining rapidly what would be the trend of births in the long run in a population which maintained indefinitely the frequencies on which the reproduction rate is based. For it may be shown that in the absence of migration the number of births in such a population would eventually come to grow at a rate indicated by the reproduction rate and by the "true rate of natural increase" derived from it. The mathematical analysis required to prove this statement is, of course, to be found mainly in Dr. Lotka's work.

In order to compute a reproduction rate, it is thus necessary to select frequencies which if they were maintained in a population would be sufficient to determine completely the number of births. For example, age specific fertility rates and mortality rates of women, the frequencies on which the traditional net reproduction rate is based, are sufficient for this purpose. But frequencies which are sufficient may be chosen in many different ways, even from the data relating to one population at one particular time. Dr. Woofter has listed a number of the possibilities which have been suggested. Some of them are very complex. For example, the computation suggested by Hyrenius, and referred to by Dr. Woofter, amounts to calculating the rate at which births would ultimately grow in a population which permanently maintained the following frequencies: the nuptiality of men, the mortality of single men, the frequencies at which marriages of wives of each duration and each age of wife at marriage are dissolved by death or divorce, the frequencies at which marriages of each duration and each age of wife at marriage produce births, and the frequencies at which unmarried women of each age bear children. Certain other quantities also enter into the computation. The complexity of the process suggested by Hyrenius arises from the fact that he was attempting to combine fertility rates which are specific by the age of the mother or the age of the wife at marriage with the marriage rates of men. This aim may be attained by processes simpler than that used by Hyrenius. This would make it practicable to introduce other refinements. One might take the frequencies at which marriages of each duration and each number of children already born produce births within one year, and substitute them for fertility rates specific by duration and age at marriage. The other data entering into the computation might be the same as those used by Hyrenius. The material for such a computation is available for Germany. For England and Wales it will be possible to calculate fertility rates specific by all three variables (duration of marriage, parity and age of wife at marriage) when the results of the Family Census of 1946 have been fully analysed. These rates could then be used to compute a reproduction rate.

One might imagine that by combining more and more refined rates in the computation of reproductivity it would be possible eventually to arrive at the "best" reproduction rate. This, however, is not possible. Some of the reproduction rates which have been or might be computed can properly be regarded as improvements upon simpler reproduction rates. In other cases, however, we are faced with alternative reproduction rates of which it is not possible to say that one is better than the other. We can choose from among the frequencies recorded in a given time and place different systems sufficient for the computation of a reproduction rate, but no system can be said to be the correct representation of the "underlying fertility pattern" of the population. As Dr. Woofter points out, it is no use looking for a single figure to characterize the underlying pattern.

I think that the insoluble conflict between different reproduction rates might well be one of the main reasons why reproduction rates will

MODIFYING THE NET REPRODUCTION RATE: DISCUSSION

continue to be used. Every reproduction rate gives a limited indication of what would happen on a certain long run projection of births. It is particularly convenient to have such a quick method of obtaining an indication, because there are many possible ways of calculating reproduction rates and making projections. Moreover, the fact that there are different reproduction rates based on frequencies recorded in a population at a given time means that it is logically impossible for all the frequencies relevant to the number of births to remain as they are at that time. Some aspects of the "situation of the moment" must change. Reproduction rates show something about these necessary changes. Thus the traditional comparison between the crude rate of natural increase and the "true rate of natural increase" shows that if the female age specific fertility and mortality rates remain constant, the age structure of the population and the crude rate of natural increase must change. Or if the "true rates of natural increase" derived from the paternal and maternal reproduction rates differ, then the age specific fertility rates of men or those of women must change. In the first of these two examples the long run implications of the age specific rates are clearly more significant than those of the crude rates. But, as the second example shows, the comparison of reproduction rates may yield important information even when it is impossible to say that one of them is a "better" measure than the other.

A reproduction rate may be of interest even if it is not at all likely that the frequencies on which it is based will continue in operation. These frequencies may not even have been observed. For example, one may wish to work out a reproduction based on hypothetical, low death rates, which are expected to be reached in the distant future. Or again, it is of interest to show how rapidly a population would increase which permanently maintained nineteenth century fertility rates, but had present-day mortality.

There is no time to discuss certain important aspects of the use of reproduction rates, such as reproduction rates computed from data of the "stock" type or the relation of reproduction rates to the question "how far is the population of reproductive age being replaced."

It is important to note that reproduction rates are unsuited to many types of analysis. They are highly composite rates. They are based on frequencies of births and deaths differentiated by age and other factors, often also on frequencies of marriage, divorce, etc. For many purposes a single figure which summarizes such diverse information is not a suitable tool. To take a very common case, reproduction rates are not suitable for investigating the effects of the trade cycle upon demographic phenomena. The conventional net reproduction rate shows the combined effect of variations in death rates and in age specific fertility rates. More complex reproduction rates involve even more factors. Entirely different phenomena about which separate information is available are thus confused in such a way that neither of them can be separately observed, while the special advantage of the reproduction rate as an indication of long run implications is not relevant to the purpose in hand. Again reproduction rates are not adequate for answering many questions of sociological interest, such as "does one section of the population marry less frequently than another," "do they limit their families more," and so forth.

Perhaps the main consequence of looking at reproduction rates in this light is that too much attention should not be paid to them. The main task of demographic analysis is to find out what is happening to the various factors controlling population growth. The long run implications of a given situation need only be investigated occasionally. For other purposes, various types of measures other than reproduction rates should normally be used. The study of the most suitable types of measures for different purposes, for example, the measurement of differential fertility, needs to be developed. Even in investigations which use reproduction rates, careful attention should be paid to the behaviour of the frequencies on which the reproduction rates are based. In published papers these frequencies should be presented to the reader. Otherwise it is not possible to assess how far it is likely that these frequencies should be maintained or to understand what their maintenance would mean in sociological terms.

FOOTNOTE

1. A more extended discussion, which deals with the problem of reproduction rates from essentially the same point of view, may be found in "The Measurement of Reproductivity" by W.A.B. Hopkin (published as Appendix 3 of the Report of the Royal Commission on Population, London, 1949).

WASHINGTON'S STATE-WIDE SYSTEM OF CENSUS TRACTS AND CENSUS DIVISIONS

Calvin F. Schmid
University of Washington

In presenting a discussion of the new state-wide system of census tracts and census divisions for the state of Washington, I should like to consider the following points:
1. What are census tracts and census divisions?
2. What is the purpose of the state-wide tracting program?
3. Of what value are census tracts and census divisions?
4. What criteria and techniques were used in delimiting census divisions and census tracts?

I. <u>What are census tracts and census divisions</u>?

Basically there is no difference between the concepts "census tract" and "census division." In deference to the United States Bureau of the Census as well as to tradition and usage, the term "census tract" is applied to large cities and their metropolitan districts, while "census division" is used in connection with rural territory and small cities. Both census tracts and census divisions are relatively small, permanent, homogeneous areas used by the United States Bureau of the Census and other agencies in the tabulation and analysis of detailed data on population, housing, births, mortality, morbidity, employment, education, income, traffic volume, business activities, agricultural production, manufacturing, and other subjects.

As all of you know, sixty of our larger cities were divided into census tracts when the 1940 decennial census was taken. The census tract idea originated with Dr. Walter Laidlaw in the city of New York in 1906. In 1910 only eight cities—New York, Chicago, Philadelphia, Pittsburgh, Boston, Baltimore, Cleveland, and St. Louis—had census tract systems. The value of census tracts for research and administrative purposes was clearly demonstrated, and it can be seen from the above data how rapidly the idea spread.

TOOLS FOR DEMOGRAPHIC RESEARCH

In the state of Washington only the corporate city of Seattle was divided into census tracts in 1940. When the 1950 census is taken the entire state will be divided into census tracts and census divisions. Washington will be the first state in the country to be tracted in this manner. This idea no doubt will spread to other states.

II. <u>What is the purpose of a state-wide system of census tracts and census divisions</u>?

From both a research and administrative point of view the old system of election precincts is obsolete and virtually useless. The deficiencies of precincts and other similar divisions for research, planning, and administrative purposes have long been recognized, but unfortunately through inertia and indifference nothing was done to improve this situation.

(a) Election precincts in the state of Washington are subject to manipulation and change. For example, of the 2,125 minor civil divisions (almost all were election precincts) in 1940 only 1,154 or a little more than half were comparable with the 1930 minor civil divisions. This means that every ten years many hundreds of thousands of dollars are spent in compiling and tabulating valuable data on population, housing, agriculture, and other subjects merely to be discarded because of adherence to the antiquated and useless system of election precincts.

(b) Election precincts are usually laid out for political convenience and without reference to geographic, historic, social, or economic relationships. Census divisions and census tracts, on the other hand, are carefully planned and possess marked demographic, economic, and social homogeneity. Such units logically tend to become the basic points of reference for fact-collecting, administration, and research.

(c) Boundaries of election precincts are difficult, and, I might add from actual experience, frequently impossible to identify in the field. Election precincts almost invariably follow section lines and even fractional parts of sections. Because precinct boundaries are not definitive and readily identifiable, much time and effort are wasted and omissions and duplications are an inevitable consequence in field enumerating and interviewing.

III. <u>Of what value are census tracts and census divisions</u>?

The following illustrations indicate how census tracts and census divisions can be used for research and administrative purposes:

(a) <u>Governmental agencies</u> throughout the state will be able to use census tracts and census divisions for assembling and analyzing data as

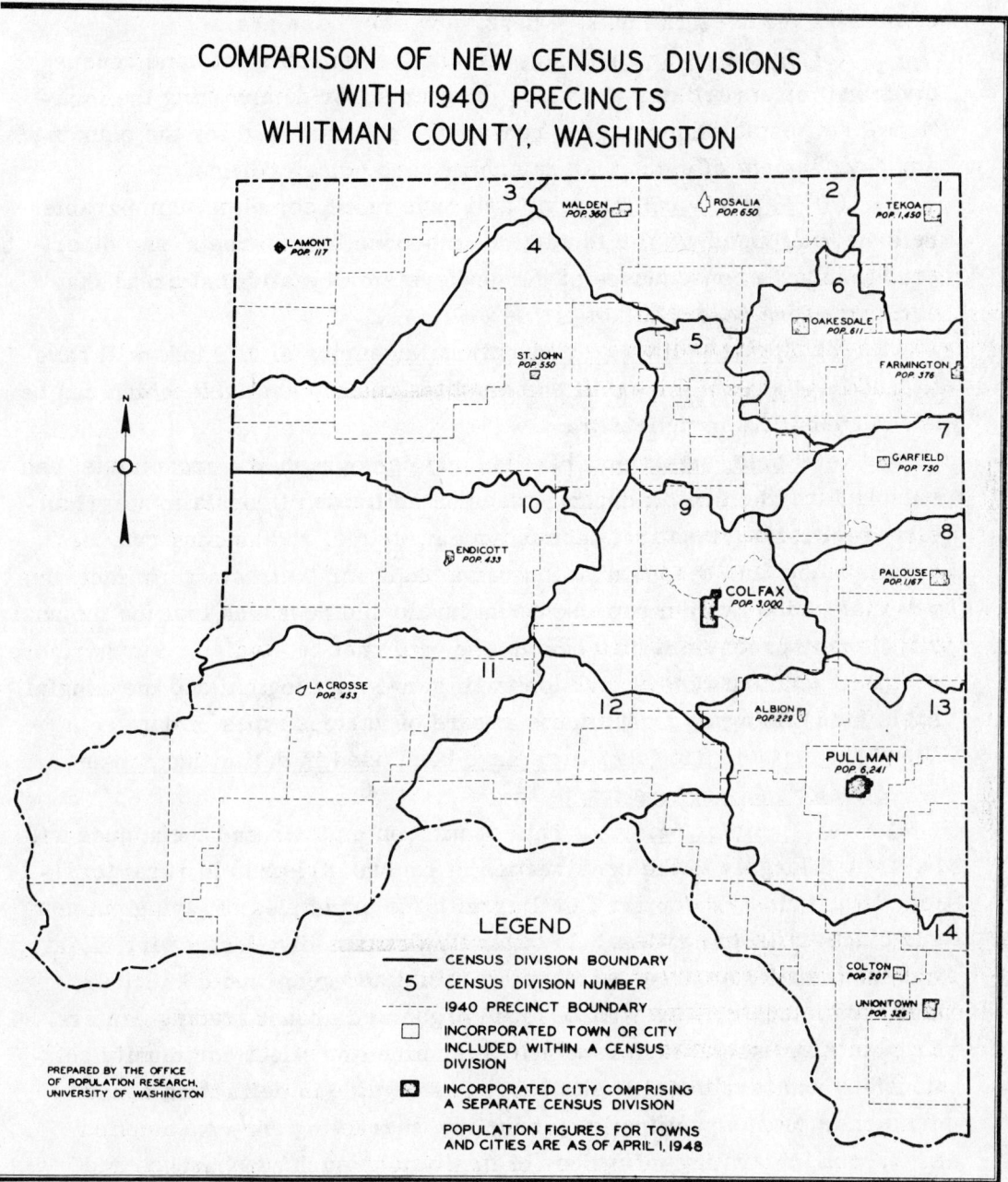

FIGURE 1

well as for various kinds of administrative work. State and county planning boards, health agencies, highway and traffic engineers, public welfare boards, law enforcement agencies, fire protection, and other governmental agencies can make extensive use of these areas.

(b) <u>Business and industry</u> can utilize census tracts and census divisions for advertising and sales programs, for determining the location of new establishments, for real estate planning, and for the planning and development of electrical, telephone, and other utilities.

(c) <u>Agricultural interests</u> will have more complete, comparable, reliable, and meaningful information on production, markets, and other conditions as a consequence of the new system of statistical areas than has heretofore been available.

(d) <u>Social welfare and educational agencies</u> of all kinds will have detailed social data for small communities readily available which can be used extensively in their work.

(e) <u>Social scientists</u>, particularly demographers, economists, and sociologists who are conducting research in fields of population, agriculture, real estate, taxation, unemployment, crime, and housing can use census tracts and census divisions as a basis for their work. In fact, this new state-wide system represents an invaluable research tool for the analysis of many problems which heretofore could not be studied. Furthermore, census tracts and census divisions will serve as a logical and meaningful basis for building up a continuous record of various types of data.

IV. <u>What criteria and techniques have been used in delimiting census divisions and census tracts?</u>[1]

(a) <u>Basic principles</u>. This section on criteria and techniques will be limited largely to the construction of census divisions in rural territory, since most of you are familiar with the principles of laying out census tracts in larger cities.[2] In delimiting census divisions every effort was made to define areas which were social and geographic entities. Ordinarily such entities will be found organized around trading centers. Economic and social factors which determine or reflect community relationships and territorial limits served as a guide in delimiting census divisions. More specifically, production, marketing and consumption areas, the integrating influences of institutions such as churches and schools, farm organizations, and farmer marketing and production organizations are illustrations of social and economic criteria that were used in constructing census divisions. Consideration was also given to significant physiographic factors which separate or in any way influence the structure or limits of a community, such as mountains, valleys, rivers, and lakes.[3]

It is recognized that the characteristics of areas delimited on the basis of these principles may change so that an integrated community at the time of initial planning may undergo marked changes subsequently. The intention is that permanency of area boundaries is of primary importance. The study of changes will be facilitated by the retention of permanent boundaries.

(b) Size. In considering the size of census divisions and census tracts, population was given primary emphasis. According to the original specifications, the average size of census divisions over the entire state was to approximate 2,000 people, while census tracts were to be appreciably larger. Actually the mean population size of census divisions and census tracts combined is 2,500. In general, the census divisions are relatively compact with respect to areal extent and of course consist of contiguous territory. No attempt was made to adhere rigidly to any set population figure, although the range of the size of census divisions has been kept within comparatively narrow limits. In certain instances where the population is extremely sparse, the number of people in a census division will be found to be comparatively small.

Incorporated and unincorporated places of 2,500 or more inhabitants each consist of one or more separate census divisions. Smaller places have been included as a part of a census division.

(c) Boundaries. The United States Bureau of the Census requires that all census division boundaries be relatively permanent and clearly defined since they must also form the limits of enumeration districts. It is also essential to have definitive and easily recognizable boundaries for research and administrative purposes. In laying out census divisions for rural territory, the following boundaries were considered acceptable unless for some reason they were known to be of a temporary character:

(1) Highways, roads, and streets,
(2) Railroads,
(3) Fire trails and other well-defined mountain trails,
(4) Rivers, streams, and lakes,
(5) Transmission lines (should not be used in farming areas where they cross over many individual farms),
(6) Canals and aqueducts, and
(7) Comparatively short projected lines between two definite points with preference given to township, range, and section lines. Boundaries of this type were kept at a minimum.

TOOLS FOR DEMOGRAPHIC RESEARCH

The names of the boundaries of census divisions were shown directly on the maps. All census divisions are laid out within county boundaries.

(d) <u>Urban Census Divisions</u>. Census divisions also have been set up for urban places except where census tracts have been established. Places of 2,500 or more inhabitants form one or more census divisions, depending upon their population. Places of less than 10,000 inhabitants have not been divided. The principles to be followed in establishing census divisions in urban places were the same as those used in setting up census tracts.

(e) <u>Numbering</u>. In order to facilitate easy reference to maps, coding guides, tabular and other data, census divisions have been identified by numbering them within each county in consecutive order in serpentine fashion beginning at the upper right hand corner.

(f) <u>Clearance and Approval</u>. In the actual process of laying out census tracts and census divisions, interested local groups of all kinds were consulted for guidance and approval. Agricultural agents, county commissioners, planning boards, road engineers, superintendents of schools, and other informed people were of the greatest assistance in the actual field work. Needless to say, an extraordinary amount of correspondence, personal and committee consultation, and field checking were necessary in carrying out this project.

After the preliminary draft of the areas was completed, county and city maps showing the numbers and boundaries of the census divisions and census tracts, together with written descriptions of the boundaries, were sent to the Bureau of the Census for checking and suggestions. Most of the maps also were reviewed by the Bureau of Agricultural Economics. The checking and reviewing process involved additional correspondence as well as extensive field work. As the project neared completion the final reviewing and checking process was done through direct personal consultation in Washington with staff members of the Bureau of the Census and the Bureau of Agricultural Economics.

(g) <u>Reporting and Publication of Census Data</u>. Population and housing data collected by the Bureau of the Census will be published for census divisions in lieu of tabulations formerly made for minor civil divisions or subdivisions of urban places. In the case of census divisions in rural territory, sub-totals for rural places included as part of a census division will be shown separately in a manner similar to the tabulations heretofore published for minor civil divisions and incorporated places.

WASHINGTON'S CENSUS TRACTS AND CENSUS DIVISIONS

Other detailed statistics on population, housing, and agriculture will be made available by census divisions on a cost basis as has been done in the past for data by minor civil divisions.

FOOTNOTES

1. Most of the material in this section has been taken from a memorandum prepared by the United States Bureaus of the Census and of Agricultural Economics and the Washington State Census Board entitled "Statistical Areas on a State-Wide Basis." The present writer, as executive secretary of the Washington State Census Board, initiated the state-wide tracting program and has had charge of the research work.

2. Calvin F. Schmid, "The Theory and Practice of Planning Census Tracts," Sociology and Social Research, Vol. XXII (January-February, 1938), pp. 228-238; Howard Whipple Green and Esther M. Wright, Census Tract Manual, United States Bureau of the Census, 1947, passim.

3. Beginning with J.M. Williams' study of An American Town in 1906 the rural sociologist has considered the community of major research significance. The concept of the rural community as defined by the "team haul" was first developed by Warren H. Wilson in his Evolution of the Country Community in 1907. It was not until 1915 when Charles J. Galpin published his famous study, The Social Anatomy of an Agricultural Community that the rural sociologist had developed any explicit and objective techniques for delimiting the rural community. Since the appearance of Galpin's monograph scores of similar studies have been conducted throughout the country.

"Rural community" has been defined as "that form of association maintained between the people and their institutions in a local area in which they live on disperse farmsteads and in a village which usually forms the center of their common activities. The rural community is composed of both farm and village people, the farm people living on dispersed farmsteads in contrast to the modern agricultural village of Europe and Asia where they live in the village. The area is defined by a boundary within which the village forms the center of the common activities of most of the families, although it is recognized. . . that there are open-country communities, particularly in the South, which have no village center. But the real community from a sociological standpoint is the form of association between these people and between their institutions in the given area."
—Dwight Sanderson, Rural Sociology and Rural Social Organization (1942), pp. 278-279.

CENSUS DIVISIONS IN THE STATE OF WASHINGTON: DISCUSSION

Clarence E. Batschelet
U. S. Bureau of the Census

The statistical areas which Dr. Schmid has described in his paper on the <u>Washington State-Wide System of Census Tracts and Census Divisions</u> have the approval of the Bureau of the Census.

Townships, precincts, and other types of minor civil divisions within counties have been used traditionally by the Bureau of the Census for purposes of enumeration control in census taking and for the presentation of statistics for small local areas. In some States, the minor civil divisions used have served the purpose satisfactorily. In other States, particularly where election precincts or other areas that are not permanently established or not widely known locally have been used, there have been problems. The deficiencies of precincts and certain other similar divisions for research, planning, and administrative purposes have long been recognized by the Bureau of the Census. In some States, the boundaries of these areas are subject to frequent change so that in many cases it is not possible to compare data from one period to another. In addition, the boundaries of these areas are very often difficult to identify in the field. Besides being relatively impermanent and difficult to identify, precincts and other similar divisions are usually laid out for political convenience and without reference to geographic, historic, social or economic relationships.

In order to improve and facilitate the basis for enumerating and analyzing data, the Bureau of the Census initiated a field survey in certain States in 1947 in order to determine if any organizations or local groups would be interested in establishing permanent areas which could be used in lieu of the unstable county subdivision for which statistics had previously been published. In the State of Washington, the Census Board manifested an interest in this project and indicated a willingness to assume the responsibility of laying out permanent areas in the various counties of the State, following the principles which had been drawn up jointly by the

CENSUS DIVISIONS IN THE STATE OF WASHINGTON: DISCUSSION

Bureau of the Census, the Bureau of Agricultural Economics, and the Washington State Census Board. The census divisions, as established under this program, will be used by the Bureau of the Census in lieu of election precincts for the publication of the census returns. These permanent census divisions for the rural portions of the counties will serve many of the same purposes now served by census tracts in the larger metropolitan areas and, in addition, will make available a useful analytical tool for agricultural research.

SECTION III

RESOURCES FOR THE WORLD'S PEOPLE

Dinner Meeting, May 28, 1949
Conrad Taeuber, President of the Association, Presiding

POPULATION AND SCARCE FOOD RESOURCES

John D. Black
Harvard University

My function in this paper is to set the stage for a discussion of the relation of population increase to the use of the earth's food-producing resources that will cause the main factors in this relation to stand forth in their true perspective. Dr. Taeuber has organized the program for this session in such a way as to give me a chance to set these factors forth as I have come to understand them, and then for Professor Bradfield and Mr. Clapp, who know much more about soil resources and their use than I do, to reconstruct as needed what I say on these aspects of the problem, and then for the members of this Association, who know much more about population increase than I do, to revise what I say on that side of the problem. Out of this discussion it is hoped will come a much more rational statement of the problem than the public has found in such books as Vogt's Road to Survival, Osborn's Our Plundered Planet, Pearson and Harper's World Hunger, Prentice's Food, War and the Future, and Chew's Plowshares into Swords.

I also hope this discussion will set the problem in better perspective than was done at M.I.T.'s recent "Mid-Century" celebration in which our Frank Notestein engaged himself with Osborn, Vannevar Bush and others. I shall have to say that this session was unsatisfactory in that some of the more important relationships in the problem were not set forth, with the result that the three thousand spectators in that arena may well have gone away with only a distorted idea as to what the shooting was all about.

What has brought this subject to the fore at the moment is that a couple of ecologists have published confusing books that have attracted wide attention, and hence we must begin by reviewing their contributions. In my very young days when I was a high school teacher of biology, I had great hopes for the contribution which ecology might make to major world problems of this type, and even planned a career in this field at one stage.

RESOURCES FOR THE WORLD'S PEOPLE

But the ecologists of today, if we must judge them by such specimens as Vogt and Osborn, seem unable to accept man in his environment on the same basis as other forms of life. Osborn writes, it is true, that "we must be prepared to accept the concept that man, like all other living things, is part of one great biological scheme" (p. 196). It would be interesting indeed to have the ecologists really stick to such an assignment and deal with man as a biological unit competing for survival in his environment. But we do not get this from our two recent exponents of ecology. When one species, plant or animal expands to the limit of its food resources, Osborn describes this as part of the "economy of nature." But when man does the same thing, Osborn is likely to call him a destructive "geologic force." In "nature," if some natural event causes a form of life to multiply rapidly, there shortly follows an increase in numbers of the species that prey upon it, whereupon the first species is rapidly decimated, and the preying species then perish in much larger numbers. Thus "friendly," beneficent nature, à la Rousseau, keeps the forms of life in "natural balance." The white race that moved into North America and proceeded to work toward such a natural balance, is, however, condemned by Osborn and others for not passing on to the next generation an undiminished patrimony. Even today, the major obstacle to getting technologically good woodland management adopted is that the price of timber is so low, because of remaining stands of virgin timber, or more importantly, of mature or nearly mature stands that followed naturally after the virgin cutting, that such management will not pay for itself. The recent Reappraisal Report of the Forest Service tells us that the total drain in a recent year was 13.7 billion cubic feet of timber and the total growth 13.4 billion, and predicts a total drain ten years later of only 14.6 billion cubic feet. The deficit in prospect is serious only in mature or sawlog timber. The smaller and inferior trees that need to be removed to give the sawlog trees a chance to develop, often do not sell for enough to pay the cost of harvesting and marketing.

The soils situation is not so greatly different from the forest situation as is commonly supposed. In large areas in the United States, the natural stores of plant nutrients in the land, <u>subsoil plus topsoil</u>, are still so abundant that food and other farm products sell at prices so low that farmers cannot afford to replenish all the nutrients removed. Certainly this was true in much of the United States in most of the years from 1921 to 1940. Western Europe could not afford, in the latter half of the nineteenth century and until World War I, fully to replenish the nutrients

POPULATION AND SCARCE FOOD RESOURCES

in many of its fields because food could be bought so cheaply in the New World. If it did so increasingly after World War I, it was commonly at the expense of the standards of living of its people.

Highly pertinent in this connection are the remarks of Gen. Francis A. Walker, the leading American economist of his time, who became the director of the Census of 1880 and wrote as follows in his introduction to Volume III of the Agricultural Census:

> Down to this time our apparently wasteful culture has, as I have sought to show, been the true economy of the national strength; our apparent abuse of the capital fund of the country has, in fact, effected the highest possible improvements of the public patrimony. Thirty-eight noble states, in an indissoluble union, are the ample justification of this policy. Their schoolhouses and churches, their shops and factories, their roads and bridges, their railways and warehouses, are the fruits of the characteristic American agriculture of the past.
>
> But from a time not far distant, if indeed it has not already arrived, a continuance in this policy will be, not the improvement of our patrimony, but the impoverishment of our posterity.

If General Walker had been writing a preface to the Census of 1940, he might have written in precisely the same vein, again saying that the exploitation of the past had been sound national economic policy but that the point has now been reached, and so forth. Conceivably some commentator another sixty years from now will be moved to write in the same way.

The basic principles involved are simply these, that land can be maintained at different levels of productivity—some cotton lands of the South, for example, at levels giving yields all the way from 150 to 500 pounds per acre—and that at any given time, in a given state of a country's demand for food and other products of the soil, it pays to maintain the soil at a certain level of productivity. If all the cotton land in the United States were maintained at the maximum level, the supply of cotton would depress world cotton prices 6 or 8 cents a pound. There is a similar most advantageous maintenance level for Corn Belt lands. To exploit or mine them in their virgin state until well down to such a maintenance level has commonly been good national economy.

In the language of the ecologists named, the human species, habitat the United States, whenever it is working toward this _optimum_ productivity level, is simply working toward that "natural" balance in the use of resources which is the ecologist's economy of nature.

Apparently the ecologists become confused by the dollars or francs in which the human species registers its sense of relative values. After all, the dollars or francs are simply indicators of the relation between the needs for and the scarcity of different resources. Similar scales of relative values exist in non-human society, but they never get registered as a price in a market place. In consequence, there is a good chance that the resources are much less efficiently distributed among different uses in non-human than in human society.

Two differences between the economy of non-human and human society are, however, much worth noting. The first is that in non-human society, insofar as the individual animal or mating unit is concerned, the standard of value is simple biological survival, whereas in human society it includes all that goes to make up the standard of living of a people, and all their hopes and aspirations. The second is that in non-human society the values, again insofar as the individual animal or mating unit is concerned, are extremely short-run, almost day-to-day survival for the most part, whereas, except among human groups on the verge of starvation, there is much planning for the future, and weighing of present and future values against each other. There may be a grand design in nature as a whole, or some process like Darwin's "natural selection," that adapts a species better to its environment, but surely no conscious weighing of alternatives within the species.

Although human societies do look out for their futures, they may not do so well enough. Surely no one would want to affirm that all societies have done so on all occasions; or that though some society, like a nation, may have done so in the aggregate, all groups within it have done so. There are strong reasons to expect that a nation like the United States that for two centuries or more has been producing cheaply by drawing upon reserves of plant nutrients may overreach itself at some critical turning point and reduce the productivity level of its soils too far. Osborn told us at the M.I.T. celebration that this country was still taking more out of its land than it is putting back. This could be true, however, and still we may not have overreached ourselves in the aggregate.

At any rate, we need have no fear in this country of declining levels of food consumption because of past abuse of our lands—not even, as will appear presently, after allowing for all the exports other nations will buy from us. The increase of more than a third in agricultural output in this country since before the war has not, in the over-all, reduced the productivity level of our lands in any serious measure, and further increases are easily possible at lesser drains on the land than in the past, and at lower costs.

It is not sufficient, however, to deal with this subject only in terms of the national aggregate. It might well be that considerable sections of the country have overreached themselves in this respect although the nation as a whole has not. Yet even here the usual kind of mock-heroic reacting to the superficial can lead us astray. Take as an example the northeastern states which Dr. Bradfield and I know best. In the last one hundred years, close to ten million acres of land once in crops and open pasture have gone back to trees in the New England states alone, in six states with a combined surface area scarcely larger than that of Illinois. Did they go back to trees because their soils had been degraded well below their virgin levels of fertility? Not at all. Most of them never had much fertility. They were farmed successfully from first settlement until they were abandoned to trees only by putting into them almost as much plant nutrient as was taken out. When cheap cereals, meats, butter and cheese began moving in from the Midwest, the only kinds of farming that could persist in New England were those that provided highly perishable or bulky foods for the growing cities, and/or, like dairying, produced their own plant nutrients in part. Agriculturally speaking, the lands of New England still in farms are on a higher level of productivity today than when first settled. (Of course this is not true of the timberlands of New England.)

How about the piedmont and sand-hill sections of the South? What they need is a large migration off the land and a consolidation of farms into units large enough to permit diversified crop-and-livestock farming— much the same kind of a conversion as has already occurred in the Northeast. The productivity level of much of this region has probably fallen too low, and will fall still further unless strong measures are used, if the <u>present population continues to try to make a living on it</u>. But if there can be an orderly process of out-migration and consolidation, a sound balance of inputs and outgo of plant nutrients will presently be established. Cotton will still be grown in these sections, but only as a supplementary cash crop. The cotton that this country needs, plus that which is likely to find an export outlet, can, if need be, all be grown on the more level delta, upper coastal and other plain lands of the South and Southwest and the irrigated lands of the West, following systems of farming that almost necessarily maintain economic productivity levels if they are to be profitable.

This same description fits much of the rolling terrain of the border states and reaching up into south central Iowa, and southern Illinois, Indiana and Ohio.

As for the semi-arid reaches of the Great Plains, it seems probable that considerable natural range land has been converted into cropland that will suffer so much from wind erosion in dry series of years that the nation cannot afford to have it kept in crops.

The foregoing raises the important question of the conflict between national and individual or group interest in land use. There may be large values to the nation, because its balancing of present and future is indefinite in span, that are not of great moment to a particular generation of individual operators. Given such a difference, the nation <u>can afford to make investments in the future</u> that an individual cannot; and it should always be prepared to do this. But it is also true that a nation can easily make <u>unnecessary and costly investments in the future</u>. It surely would make many such investments if it allowed itself to be stampeded by every group that sees the nation's natural reserves of some resource being "depleted." Even such an investment as that intended to insure a future supply of saw-timber should be carefully analyzed from this point of view.

Perhaps a case in point is investment in saving from erosion the sacrosanct "topsoil" of the ultra-conservationists. Osborn tells us that it takes nature, under the most favorable circumstances, "anywhere from 300 to 1000 years or more to build a single inch of topsoil" (p.51). If this were all of the story, no nation could afford to let any land with a slope of more than one or two per cent ever be planted to a cultivated crop. Yet civilizations have been doing this since earliest history, and if any have perished, it has been for other primary reasons, Simkovitch's <u>Hay and History</u> and Osborn and Vogt to the contrary. Given a sufficient depth of ordinary subsoil, a rotation system that keeps the land in broadcast crops or grass and legumes four years out of five, supplemented by barnyard manure or winter cover crops, will ordinarily keep a sufficient depth of good topsoil on slopes up to five per cent, especially if the cultivated crop is farmed on the contour. The depth and character of the subsoil are more important over the centuries than the topsoil.

Discussion of land use in terms of "conservation" is always in danger of leading us astray because of the confusion in the public mind as to the definition of conservation. We are safer if we analyze it in terms of the economics of land management, first, from the standpoint of the individual operator, and then from the standpoint of the nation. When we do this, more often than not we come to the happy result that the system of land management that pays an owner-operator best is one that also accords with the longer-term public interest. It simply does not pay a farmer to let the productivity level of his farm fall very far below the optimum level. On virgin soils of high natural fertility, such as the prairie soils of the Corn Belt, or the chernozems of the Plains, this may permit taking more out of the soil than is put back for several decades, but not elsewhere. Except in such areas, the farm that is running down, as a result of heavy cropping and no replacement of plant nutrients, or from excessive erosion, declines in profitability within five to ten years.

A positive form of statement of this same proposition may be more meaningful. Take any farm at random anywhere in the United States and work out for the owner a plan with its operator that promises to maximize its net return over a five or ten-year span, and the chances are at least four out of five that this plan will build up rather than lessen the productivity of the farm.

We at Harvard have just finished testing out this proposition on 239 dairy farms averaging 225 acres in 14 areas in the six New England states. The plans worked out with the farmers promise to increase the net farm income by exactly one half. They call for only a 2 per cent increase in the acres in crops, and for improving, by fertilization and seeding to better grasses and clovers, and a little clearing away of brush and stones, an additional 17 acres of pasture land per farm and 11 acres of hay land. The average forage production of these farms will be increased from 135 to 192 tons, the number of milk cows from 24 to 31, and the production of milk per cow from 6700 to 7400, with a 5 per cent decrease in purchased grain per cow. An average of 98 acres of woodland per farm put under simple and not very intensive management will double in output and return 40 per cent more per man-day of labor.

Could the productivity of these farms be raised still further? Very easily. Then why do not the plans provide for this? Because the market for the milk would absorb a larger volume only at too low prices. The productivity level designed for these farms is the optimum as defined earlier. Perhaps it needs to be added that this optimum has been rising on the better lands of New England for the past fifty years.

A similar analysis in most parts of the United States would show closely parallel results. Nearly everywhere the limit on improved management would be set by the market for the farm products.

While the foregoing accurately describes the prevailing situation in the United States, thousands of farms in almost any large block of counties are suffering serious loss of productivity at any given time. A large fraction of these are farms rented under leases that in effect offer inducements to tenants to abuse them. Another large fraction are farms too small, especially if size is measured in net product, to finance needed improvements or additions to capital. Others are farms operated by men too old to make improvements. It is highly important for the country and its people that the losses from all of these sources be checked. It is for this reason that we economists support vigorously our present so-called "conservation" programs—not because we are fearful of world hunger.

Now let us turn back to the population side of our assignment. It should now be obvious that any population that has been predicted by responsible analysts for the United States is going to have a clear opportunity to achieve higher levels of food consumption. How much higher will depend upon the balance between the rate of improvement in the arts of production and the rate of population growth, and upon how evenly the purchasing power for food is distributed among our people. Given a high relative gain in the arts, with no gain in evenness of distribution, and this country will find itself exporting increasing amounts of food over the centuries. With more even distribution at the same time, our people will shift consumption more to foods of livestock origin, and this will tend to check exports.

The first point to make as we turn to the rest of the world is that we must not let ourselves be drawn into the common mistake of thinking of this problem in terms of balancing world totals of prospective food supply against world totals of prospective population, as is so generally done these days. I know of no way of designating this approach to the problem any better than to call it the "common trough" approach—that is, thinking of the human race as a vast drove of hogs feeding out of one common trough. My Harvard colleague Karl Sax was thinking in these terms when in an article in Science, later reproduced in the Congressional Record, he figured that 2 1/2 acres of cropland is needed to feed an average person properly, and that the world has less than this now; also Director Dodd of FAO when he recently told the world that somewhere within it 57,000 new mouths are sitting down to breakfast each morning.

As I stated in a paper before the American Economic Association last December, the social scientist approaches this problem like all others in terms of existent or potential social units or aggregates. For some phases of the population-food supply relationship, the nation is the appropriate aggregate; for others, segments of nations, such as our own South, or the Maritime Provinces of Canada. For certain aspects of this problem, the aggregate will be as small as the group of Spanish-Americans

POPULATION AND SCARCE FOOD RESOURCES

living in the upper Rio Grande Valley of New Mexico. In analyzing the relationship of population to food supply, the underlying issue in the social scientist's approach is whether, for any one such social aggregate, <u>the rate of improvement in the arts is as fast as, or faster, than the rate of population increase</u>. If the rate for the arts is faster than that for the population, standards of living are almost sure to be rising, except that temporarily, as in Russia in some recent decades, and in much of Europe just now, the gains may be diverted to capital formation.

The arts in any such balancing are not merely the agricultural arts. For a nation to increase its aggregate or per-capita industrial output so as to be able to import more food may be as effective as to increase its food-fibre output per worker on its farms; and likewise to improve its transport facilities so as to handle food and other products more effectively.

The social aggregate that is most important for us to consider in this connection is sometimes called "the Western Trading Bloc." It includes the United States, Western Europe and all the exporting countries that supply Western Europe with food and fibre in sizeable volume.

For population and food-supply analysis, however, it is not sufficient to define such aggregate solely in terms of exchange of goods — exchange of populations also enters into it. Europe may accept the sugar, fats and oils, rubber and tea of the East Indies and Southeast Asia; but it does not accept its peoples as immigrants. Consequently these Eastern countries have to work out by themselves, in the main, their own balances of increases in the arts and increases in population. They are not part of the same social aggregate so far as population relationships are involved, as are Western Europe, the United States, Canada, Latin America, Australia, New Zealand and South Africa.

What happens, it follows, to the balance of population and food supply in India or China, to be specific, has very little direct bearing on that balance in the United States, or in France, or Sweden, or even the United Kingdom. There may come a time when exchange of foods and other products and of populations, between North America or Western Europe and the Far East, will be free enough so that the balance of rates in increase in the arts and in population in one of this pair figures importantly in standards of living in the other. But that day is still far removed. Efforts of FAO and the other units in the United Nations should be directed toward hastening that day, but other more important objects must not be sacrificed for this one.

RESOURCES FOR THE WORLD'S PEOPLE

As for the general argument that the countries with good diets should share their food with the peoples of the densely populated regions, one has only to point out that if they had done this in the past three hundred years, most of them would now be down close to the Malthusian level of subsistence. The hope of the world is in the countries that have escaped such a fate and that can now help the rest of the world to escape from it. And if these fortunate countries are not to dissipate their precious chance to help, they must guard carefully against measures that may seem helpful on the surface but in the end will only drag them down toward the Malthusian level. And the Malthusian countries must guard equally carefully against permitting such mistakes to be made ostensibly in their behalf.

How much of the world is already at the stage where its arts are advancing faster than its population? Howard Tolley considered this point in a paper read before the American Academy for the Advancement of Science in December, 1946, recently published in a symposium, "Freedom From Want,"[1] and concluded that only forty per cent of the earth's human population is now living in countries which on the average have reached this stage. The progress of humanity toward a goal of food enough for all, it is pointed out in another paper in this same symposium, is measured by the number and size of the population groups that are added to this forty per cent. The forty per cent which Mr. Tolley mentioned will become fifty per cent in a few decades, then sixty per cent, etc. How long before countries like China and India will start on their way toward this optimum? They are likely to rise from their present levels rather slowly at the start—even if they make mighty strides in agricultural technology and industrialization. The gains for a few decades will mainly take the form of less disease and misery, and longer, healthier lives. The accompanying rise in the ratio of production to maintenance rations in their diets will presently, however, begin to manifest itself in rising levels of living, and this in a few decades in declining birthrates. Unless this stage is presently reached, the gains will be lost and the countries will start backwards and downwards again away from their optima.

The reader may be objecting at this point to putting all of Western Europe in one social aggregate, and all of Latin America. What about Spain's progress in the arts? And Puerto Rico's? Logically there is no difference between grouping these with the rest of Europe and of North America, and considering the United States or Canada as all one aggre-

-60-

POPULATION AND SCARCE FOOD RESOURCES

gate. Spain, like the South within the United States, and Quebec within Canada, is a sub-aggregate within a larger one. The sub-aggregates work out their own balances between population growth and the arts more or less as do nations or groups of nations. Generally, however, the institutional concomitants are different. Thus exchange of food and other products is almost certain to be freer within a nation than among nations; and more important, population movements are freer. As long, however, as important differences in man-land ratios, in output per worker, and in levels of living, persist among provinces or regions within a country, separate social sub-aggregates exist.

The foregoing suggests the query as to how progress in the population-food-supply balance occurs within such aggregates. The answer is that generally it does not take the form of raising the average level of the whole group at one time. Instead it mainly takes the form of accretions to the groups of families that have already been able to raise their levels of living by keeping the numbers in their families adjusted to their abilities to feed, clothe and educate them. Even the so-called Malthusian countries have considerable blocks of families that have made this adjustment. These blocks are expanding. Sometimes, however, progress in this direction is greatly aided in particular areas by a sudden increase in output and earnings arising from new industries, land developments, technologies and the like. Commonly in such situations only part of the families sink all their gains in the feeding of more mouths. Also out-migration from a region can be large enough to help importantly—it was in the case of Ireland, Norway and other countries of Europe in the 19th century. Ordinarily, however, it helps much the families that migrate and very little those left behind.

What about the balance of food supply and population in this Western Trading Bloc? The evidence of history is clear that diets began to improve not long after industrialization took firm hold in any country in this Bloc. The populations were able not only to buy more and better food in exchange for the factory products which they turned out with the aid of power and machinery, but in general an agricultural revolution accompanied the industrial revolution, giving a larger food output per man-day of agricultural labor. There seems to have been a brief period, however, from 1900 to around 1919, when the population within this Bloc was increasing faster than the food supply. At any rate, prices of food rose more rapidly in this period than most other prices. Much of Europe at this time was at the stage of industrialization when the population gains very rapidly. There is considerable evidence that the turn would have come as early as 1915-16 except for the first World War. From 1920 to the second World War, the arts of food and fibre production kept fully up with, and surely exceeded in some years, the population growth in this group of nations. As for losses from erosion and exploitation of plant nutrients, most of Western Europe has been farmed for centuries in ways that maintain a relatively high level of productivity. The strong shift toward more forage crops and livestock in the last hundred years has contributed importantly to this result.

The sensible report to make on conservation as a phase of the food-supply-population ratio in this part of the world is therefore that so far as the social aggregate that includes the United States and Western Europe is concerned, the management of its farm lands <u>could</u> easily be heedless enough of the future to reduce the levels of food consumption in the next fifty or one hundred years; but, barring further destructive wars, it would have to be almost unbelievably bad to lead ultimately to mass hunger. The reasonable expectation is that the management will improve rather than retrograde.

This is the point at which to tie in Vannevar Bush's analysis of the possibilities of producing foods by new processes to be developed by science. The check on these is competition from food produced by improvement of present forms of agriculture. Let these improvements within the Western Trading Bloc fail to advance the arts of production as fast as the population, so that food prices begin to rise relatively, and we need have no doubt that science will develop new processes, first, of fertilizer production, and then if need be, of more nearly direct food production.

It is fortunate for the human race that scientific developments in this field are thus held in check. Of what value, on earth or in heaven, would be the new multitides that could be fed if science were to produce the wonders in food production that its ardent disciples threaten us with? There are already too many people for good living in the Northeastern part of the United States.

We are on less secure ground when we start talking about the so-called Malthusian countries. Most of what follows is largely speculative. In such societies, everybody works who is in the least able, but most of them have too little strength, because of their low food intake, for more than a few hours of real work per day. A balance is reached between the amount of work and the food resulting at the point which supports the <u>maximum number</u> of persons, taking into account the additional food needed to bring children into the world and rear them to the point where they produce more than they eat.

The principal factor qualifying the foregoing analysis is the unequal distribution of property and income. The analysis is exactly true only if these are distributed absolutely equally. If there is a landlord class, or any group in society which lives without working, this group becomes an additional burden on those who work, and the population numbers are reduced to that extent.

Population is reduced in such a situation by another important factor. Not all workers in such a society produce the same amount. Some are always more capable or more efficient than others. These are able to handle more and better land and other resources than their neighbors, feed and clothe themselves better and rear more and better children. Only the families with the lowest possible, or marginal, efficiency live at the bare minimum described above. The more efficient families deprive the marginal families of the better land and other resources, and by so doing probably reduce the total population.

For two important reasons, therefore, under actual conditions even in the Malthusian areas, the population is smaller than the theoretical maximum, and the levels of living _average_ a little above the bare minimum.

Rarely do we recognize how inefficient and wasteful of resources and of human effort is a Malthusian society. The ratio of the maintenance to production rations is unbelievably high in such a society. If we assume that the growing child in India at 12 years reaches the point where it produces more than it eats, and allow as need be for those who die between birth and 12 years, only a short span of productive years is left with an average expectancy at birth of 27 years — probably not much more than 20 years. To the maintenance ration must be added, of course, the food consumed in prenatal growth and in growth until death of those dying under 12 years of age. And a large fraction of those of working ages have little left in their diets over and above maintenance rations to convert to useful work.

Clearly, it follows from the foregoing, that with no changes in the arts, a different distribution of age-specific death rates, or fewer births and longer lives, by increasing importantly the ratio of productive to unproductive years, could easily give larger populations in some Malthusian countries than many of them now have. A reducing of death rates with improved disease control will have the same general effect. However, the slope of the production function in the agriculture of the country—how much an additional man-day of labor will add to the food supply in an already overcrowded land—becomes highly pertinent at this point.

Also pertinent is the fact that in only a few corners of the earth are absolutely no improvements in the agriculture possible. In India, to cite a familiar example, nothing more than the development of a fertilizer industry would increase crop yields greatly. These improvements make possible additional working years per person which will add more to the product than to consumption. This tends to increase the number of persons who can survive. But if this increase is only in the number of persons born and surviving until the tenth year, let us say, it will induce an offsetting reduction in the efficiency of agriculture in sustaining population numbers.

The foregoing statements are mostly more or less hypothetical and need to be tested against the facts of population history. They much need to be verified in a society of nations that is now concerning itself seriously with the problems of the "underdeveloped countries."

A fitting conclusion to these offerings is the statement that obviously no understanding person will ever ask the question: Can the earth feed its growing populations? The answer can be nothing else but "Yes." If it does not feed them, how can they grow?

The question to ask instead is: <u>How large an increase in population will the potential food supply sustain</u>? The answer to this question will vary by countries and by social aggregates, and will depend upon the rate of increase in the arts and of the rise in the standard of living. The increase in the arts will depend on the kind of management that is given to the land, the level of productivity at which it is maintained, and the returns it yields per man-day of current labor and labor stored up in capital. The rise of the standard of living may or may not keep up with the increase in the arts. If it does not, population growth results. But it is also possible for standards of living to rise faster than the population.

In conclusion, more than upon anything else will the total population of the earth depend upon the rate at which the different countries, and sub-aggregates and groups within countries, reach the stage at which the arts begin to advance faster than the population and standards of living begin to rise. Industrialization, as Notestein has clearly shown, can contribute importantly to the attainment of this stage. But so can improvements in the arts of food production; also control of malaria and other diseases; and above all, education. The society of nations cannot afford to neglect any form of effort that will hasten the arrival of any nation at this auspicious stage.

FOOTNOTE

1. P. 218 ff., Vol. II, No. 4, <u>Chronica Botanica</u>, Waltham, Mass.

SOIL RESOURCES AND THE WORLD'S POTENTIAL FOOD SUPPLY

Richard Bradfield
Cornell University

The subject we are discussing in this paper is so broad, and involves so many unknowns that it is not surprising that there are wide differences of opinion about it. As I have read the views of different authors I have made an observation which I think may have some significance. In the great majority of cases the most optimistic views of the world's potentialities for sustained and increased food production are expressed by the agricultural scientists and the most pessimistic views by the non-agriculturalists! The most recent examples to come to my attention are two articles published in the Science News Letter on March 26 and April 2. The paper by Aldous Huxley, the distinguished British author, exudes pessimism from every page. That of Sir John Russell, retired Director of Rothamsted, the world's oldest and most famous Agricultural Experiment Station, an acknowledged leader among Soil Scientists for the last generation, a man who has probably seen first-hand as much of the world's agriculture as any agriculturalist now living, is, on the contrary, full of hope. This is in spite of the fact that he has been living for years on a British austerity diet!

Much misinformation has appeared in the popular press in recent years about soils. I would like to comment briefly on some of their characteristics.

Soils are derived from a mixture of powdered rock and plant and animal residues by a complex series of chemical reactions. Most rocks contain all the elements essential for the production of crops except nitrogen. The outer shell of the earth's crust is similar in chemical composition to the igneous rocks at the surface to a depth of at least 10 miles. The depth of unconsolidated rock material under the soil varies enormously, from a few inches to several hundred feet. Most extensive areas of arable soils are underlain with great depths of unconsolidated material. Eighty percent of the atmosphere above the surface of the earth is composed of

SOIL RESOURCES AND THE WORLD'S POTENTIAL FOOD SUPPLY

nitrogen. This amounts to about 1700 pounds over every square foot of the earth's surface, water as well as land. The amount of nitrogen in an acre of good topsoil to plow depth is about equal to that contained in the atmosphere over two square feet of the soil's surface.

This soil, upon which so much depends, is then a thin layer from a few inches to a few feet thick, sandwiched in between the rest of the earth's crust and the atmosphere. The earth's crust contains for all practical purposes an inexhaustible supply of all known plant nutrients except nitrogen. The atmosphere contains an inexhaustible supply of nitrogen! It is obvious then that we are not going to run out of raw materials for soil building in the foreseeable future. Many of our most important food crops cannot, however, utilize this inexhaustible supply of nitrogen in the air directly. It must first be converted into organic matter and stored in the soil. Under natural conditions from 15-30 pounds of nitrogen are added to each acre of soil each year and stored there in the form of soil organic matter or humus. In the case of leguminous crops, which have symbiotic bacteria on their roots which are capable of taking free nitrogen from the air and converting it into organic forms, the rate of storage of nitrogen can be stepped up to from 100 to 250 pounds per acre per year. Many abandoned fields will gain from 30-60 pounds of nitrogen per acre per year. Under natural conditions the rate of accumulation of nitrogen and organic matter greatly exceeds the rate of loss, hence such soils gradually increase in organic matter content. When a soil is plowed and planted to a cultivated crop the rate of oxidation of the organic matter is accelerated. If planted year after year to such soil depleting crops the amount of nitrogen available for each successive crop becomes less and less and finally reaches a level about equal to current additions of nitrogen brought down by the rain or fixed by non-symbiotic organisms from the atmosphere. Much of the land in the over-populated lands with an under-developed agriculture is being operated at this level. Yields of 8-12 bushels of corn or wheat per acre result. Such soils may differ very little in over-all total chemical composition from a very productive soil. If such "rundown lands" are allowed to "run wild" for a few years and then planted back to the same crop a greater yield is usually obtained. If the farmer will come to nature's assistance and plant a leguminous sod crop, the rate of restoration can be greatly accelerated. In fact a good crop of clover or alfalfa will often leave enough nitrogen in the soil for a 60-75 bushel corn crop. In many cases the soil may be so depleted that lime or phosphate or some other element must be added from the outside in the form of manure or commercial fertilizer before a satisfactory crop of legumes can be grown.

We see then that natural processes of soil building did not stop when agriculture started but are operating all the time. When the farmer accelerates, as he must, the destruction of organic matter by the growth of inter-tilled crops he must accelerate the soil building processes correspondingly if yields are to be permanently maintained. This is one of the primary objectives of a good crop rotation: to balance soil depleting with soil building crops. The introduction of a good rotation would in many large areas of the world, at least double the yield of many crops.

A certain amount of erosion is probably essential if we are to gain access to the inexhaustible supplies of minerals in the subsoil. We still have much to learn before we can take full advantage of the inexhaustible supplies of minerals in the subsoils beneath our feet. Modern industry and transportation have placed other potent soil building techniques at the disposal of farmers.

Fifty years ago, Sir William Crookes, then President of the British Association for the Advancement of Science, pointed out that a practical way of converting atmospheric nitrogen into fertilizer was necessary if the world was to avoid hunger. This production problem has been solved in most of the industrially developed countries. As we shall see later, however, the contribution that an unlimited supply of cheap nitrogen fertilizers can make to the food production of the world is appreciated by but few people.

In addition to the reserves of minerals in the subsoil we have enormous reserves of many of the more important of these minerals in concentrated form which have been segregated out in previous geological ages of weathering. A high proportion of the soils of the humid regions have lost a high proportion of their lime and have become acid. To obtain satisfactory growth of many crops this calcium must be restored and the acidity reduced. Fortunately, the lime needed for this purpose is available in almost unlimited quantities throughout the world. It is so widely distributed that most of our well developed agricultural regions have supplies adequate for several centuries reasonably close at hand. A few large and important areas are not so fortunate.

In a similar manner some of the phosphorus removed from the rocks in earlier stages of weathering was deposited in prehistoric seas and is now available in many huge depsoits. Salter[1] estimates that known reserves are adequate to meet the needs of agriculture, at eight times the present rate of consumption, for over five thousand years. This includes only known reserves. There is a high degree of probability that the actual

SOIL RESOURCES AND THE WORLD'S POTENTIAL FOOD SUPPLY

reserves are much larger. In many regions farmers can increase their yields of crops by the application of potash fertilizers. The supply of potash in the soil is much larger in porportion to crop needs than the content of phosphoric acid. As a matter of fact, the top three feet of the soils of the state of New York contain more potash than all of the known deposits of soluble potash salts in the United States. In spite of these large reserves in the soil many New York farmers find it profitable to use fairly large applications of soluble potash fertilizers on certain crops when grown on certain soils.. The known reserves of water soluble potash salts are sufficient to meet the needs of world agriculture on the expanded basis, which I shall discuss later, for at least 500 years. This envisages a utilization about 18 times the present rate.

Many other elements are required by plants but the quantities required are so small that the problem of supply does not seem to present any great difficulties.

The yields of crops actually obtained by farmers seldom reflect the maximum potentialities of their soil. To take full advantage of these potentialities it is necessary to have the proper temperature, the proper amount of sunlight, an adequate supply of water, etc. In addition, the seed planted must be of a variety that is well adapted to the soil and climate, the competition of weeds must be eliminated, damage to the crop by insects and diseases must be prevented. All of these factors are important. If any one of them is neglected yields will not reflect the potentialities of the soil. More information has been obtained in all of these fields in the past twenty years than in all the preceding centuries of the history of agriculture. But even so, research workers in these various fields will tell you that we have not yet even scratched the surface.

Drought is the most frequent cause of crop failures and famines. Irrigation increases yields and makes crop production less hazardous. The potentialities of supplemental irrigation in humid regions have not yet been adequately explored. From the limited experience available in this country, it is evident, however, that they are really enormous. The amount of supplementary water required is in most cases very small. Many examples could be cited of yields being boosted from 50 to 100 percent by the application of only 5 or 6 inches of water. A very high percentage of the rich alluvial soils along our rivers and smaller streams are potentially irrigable and in many cases at a relatively low cost. Much of the world could be freed from periodic drought by making proper use of surplus flood waters and of underground water reserves. We are all conscious of the great contribution that Florida and California are making to our diets. Did it ever occur to you, however, that the agriculture of Florida would be impossible without commercial fertilizers and that of most of California impossible without irrigation?

It has become the custom of many evangelistic soil conservationists in recent years to lambaste the American farmer for mining the soil and despoiling our most valuable national heritage. Although there has been much mis-use of our soil resources in this country, I think the American farmer has some remarkable achievements to his credit, achievements which have meant, and will continue to mean, more to us, and to the world at large, than is commonly appreciated. In no other country does the average farmer feed so many people, thus freeing from 80-85 percent of the population for other activities.

For the five crop years beginning in 1942, our farmers produced enough food each year to feed approximately 50 million more people than could have been fed at comparable dietary levels from our national production during the last five years of the 1930's. This remarkable production record was achieved with 10 percent fewer workers and with a shortage of machinery, fertilizer and other essential supplies. But remarkable as this achievement was, it should not be concluded that it represents our maximum economic potentialities.

The average yield of corn in several of the leading cornbelt states was approximately 60 bushels per acre in 1948. This is approximately double the average yield of this section twenty years ago. But does it represent potentialities? A cursory survey will show that 100 bushel yields of corn have become a commonplace with better farmers throughout that entire area. Yields of from 125-150 bushels are becoming more common, yields of over 200 bushels per acre have been attained, and many have set 300 bushels per acre as their goal. These production records can be matched in many other sections of the country. Perhaps the most dramatic advances have been made in the South. In most of the southern states the average yield of corn was between 15-20 bushels per acre twenty-five years ago. At the present time, with better adapted hybrids, closer planting, better tillage practices, better rotations and more adequate fertilization, yields of over 100 bushels per acre are being obtained by hundreds of the better farmers in this area. If hundreds of the better farmers can do it today thousands of them can do it tomorrow.

Cotton has made equally spectacular gains throughout most of the South. The 1948 Annual Report of the Arkansas Agricultural Experiment

SOIL RESOURCES AND THE WORLD'S POTENTIAL FOOD SUPPLY

Station states that the same amount of cotton is now being produced in Arkansas as was produced twenty years ago, but that it is being produced on half the acreage that was used at that time. If half the former cotton acreage can be freed for the production of soil building forage crops, her livestock industry can be expanded and systems of soil management developed which will control erosion and make a prosperous and permanent system of agriculture possible.

Some of the most spectacular progress has been made by the potato growers. A few years ago the average yield of potatoes in the United States was under a 100 bushels per acre. Now it frequently approaches twice that figure. Maine and Long Island have frequently had average yields of 300 bushels per acre. The better farmers of Maine, Long Island and other important producing areas are, however, frequently reporting yields of 500 and even 600 bushels per acre. The last Annual Report of the Pennsylvania Agricultural Experiment Station reports that new varieties of potatoes were tried in twelve counties in 1948. The _average_ yield was 630 bushels per acre. Individual yields of over 1000 bushels per acre were obtained. What the Experiment Stations and the better farmers can do today, the average farmer can do tomorrow! With such yields is it any wonder that Uncle Sam had to buy a high proportion of the 1948 crop at a cost of over $200,000,000 to the taxpayer in order to maintain guaranteed support prices?

We have made less progress in improving our forage crop yields in this country than with any other major crop and the potentialities for improvement are probably greater still. So much for crop production potentialities in the United States.

Now, let us take just a quick glance at potentialities for improving livestock production in this country. The average dairy cow in the United States is producing about 5,000 pounds of milk per year. Many of our better herds are averaging over 10,000 pounds and exceptional animals have produced about twice this amount. When one considers that about half of the energy in the food consumed by the average cow is used for maintenance, and only 50 percent is available for usable products, milk or meat, it is obvious that economy of production requires higher production. With artificial insemination it is now possible to rapidly improve the production of the dairy herds of the country at a rate several times the rate possible with natural methods of breeding. Enormous economies in feed utilization for livestock production can be brought about by the elimination of excessive fattening of beef cattle and hogs. Morrison[2] cites evidence that 1,700,000 cattle could be fattened in this country on the corn which is now used to put surplus fat, which is not utilized for human food, upon beef cattle. As a result of the improvement in quality and the lowering of the price of vegetable oils there is much less demand for lard now than there was a quarter century ago. In recent months, finished lard has been available on the retail market for less than the live weight of hogs on our central markets. Under such conditions, it is evident that it is not economical to feed hogs to such excessive weights and that much more lean meat could be produced with the same amount of feed if this excessive fattening were avoided.

In other parts of the world, the potentialities for improving livestock production are even greater than in this country. In many places, rinderpest is taking an enormous toll. In other regions otherwise well adapted to livestock production the Tsetse fly makes livestock production impossible. Other insect pests, also greatly reduce the productivity of livestock in tropical countries. Promising methods of dealing with all of these pests have been developed within the last few years and there is little question but that by pooling information now available and by a relatively small investment, these pests can be largely eliminated.

There are some who question the importance of livestock in the better fed world. Their views are based on the idea that it takes five or six times as much grain to support a man if converted into livestock products as would be required if the grain were consumed directly. This, of course, applies only to the portion of the feed of the animal derived from grain. Much of the livestock produced in the world is produced without any grain whatsoever. On all farms there is available a large amount of material which cannot be consumed by human beings, but which does make satisfactory feed for appropriate types of livestock. In such cases the animal is an economical means of converting these by-product materials into a highly prized food product. Much land is not suited for the growth of grain crops. It can produce, however, large quantities of grass and the grazing animals can convert this otherwise waste material into meat, wool or milk. The experience of Europe and of the United States indicates however, that there is a real place for livestock on the average farm, even when it is all tillable. Many soils tend to deteriorate in physical condition, organic matter content and possibly in other respects when planted year after year to annual food crops. If such soils are seeded down to a grass-legume mixture for a few years and "rested" from the plow their physical condition and productivity are often almost miraculously improved. Live-

SOIL RESOURCES AND THE WORLD'S POTENTIAL FOOD SUPPLY

stock are able to convert the forage thus produced into milk and meat. If the animal manure is carefully handled and returned to the soil, the soil is improved almost as much as if the crop were left unharvested on the ground. The available evidence indicates that the production of livestock is likely to continue to play an important role in food production in all of the areas where the density of population will permit the luxury of better living which we have come to associate with an abundant supply of milk, butter, cheese, eggs and meat.

One of the most intensive efforts ever made by a modern nation to increase its food production is now being made in Great Britain. Their present goal represents an expansion of 50 percent compared with pre-war and of 15 percent compared with the wartime peak of 1943-44. They hope to reach this goal by the summer of 1952. There is little question in the minds of any of the agricultural specialists but that this goal is a perfectly feasible one. The only doubt that I have heard expressed was regarding the time limit. If it was a ten year goal it would unquestionably be quite easy. The Ministry of Agriculture feels in view of their wartime achievements that it is perfectly possible by 1952.

In the beginning of the 18th century, Great Britain had a peasant type of agriculture and yields of all of the principal crops were as low as they are in the countries of eastern Europe at the present time. Good farming has restored the productivity of these soils and raised the average yield to among the highest levels attained in any country in the world. A 50 percent increase on an agriculture at that high level of development is indeed an important achievement. I am certain that it would be much easier, agronomically, to increase the production of most of our agriculturally backward countries 200 percent than it would to increase the production of Great Britain by 50 percent. Given the necessary time, capital and technical skills, however, there is no reason why the accomplishments of British and American farmers cannot be duplicated in practically all of the under-developed countries of the world having similar soil and climatic conditions.

Many people have the impression that high yields per acre deplete soils much more rapidly than low yields. It is true, of course, that a 100 bushel crop of corn will remove more fertility from an acre of soil than will a 25 bushel crop. It will not however, remove as much fertility per bushel as the 25 bushel per acre crop. Therefore, the fertility of the farm as a whole, is conserved by higher yields per acre. Higher yields require, and at the same time facilitate better all around soil management. By growing

RESOURCES FOR THE WORLD'S PEOPLE

100 bushels on one acre instead of four, the farmer can, for example, grow corn on his land only one year out of four without cutting his total corn production. This makes it possible for him to practice a good rotation, to grow for example, an acre of corn, an acre of wheat and two acres of leguminous hay crops instead of four acres of corn. With such a rotation, the soil is in a soil depleting, cultivated crop only one year in four, in a small grain crop—wheat, which is only about half as hard on the soil on the average as a corn, for one year and over half of the time it is covered with soil building leguminous sod crops. (Over half, because the leguminous sod crop is planted in the wheat and for one season grows simultaneously with it.) On average slopes, erosion control is a rather simple problem with such a rotation, contour cultivation alone will suffice in many cases. In order to grow 100 bushels of corn per acre on most soils it will be necessary to use commercial fertilizer. The forage grown would normally be fed to livestock and the manure returned to the soil. The manure, crop residues and the sod crop will normally keep up the organic matter content of the soil and will tend to keep it in good physical condition. I have stressed the importance of high yields to soil conservation because I am convinced that high yields are essential to good soil conservation in agricultural areas. Fortunately, high yields per acre also result in lower costs of production per unit of crop. This should, under a rational system of pricing react to the economic advantage of both farmer and consumer.

Thus far we have been discussing the possibility of increasing food production on land that is already being used for agriculture. Let us now consider for a few minutes the possibility of expanding agriculture into new areas. Exact information is limited but on the basis of the best evidence available, Salter[3] has pointed out that the largest areas of soil with agricultural potentialities which are not being used at present are the Podzol soils of the northern temperate zone and the Red soils of the tropics and sub-tropics. These two types of soil are estimated to occupy 28 percent of the world's land area and probably less than 1 percent of this area is now under cultivation. He estimates that there are available for development three hundred million acres of the Podzol soils in the northern temperate zone and about one billion acres of the Red tropical soils making a total area of one billion three hundred million acres of new land capable of being brought into the food production.

From my remarks up to this point you might reasonably conclude that I am convinced that there are enormous potentialities for increasing

SOIL RESOURCES AND THE WORLD'S POTENTIAL FOOD SUPPLY

the food production of the world. The physical resources are ample, the sciences of plant and animal production, imperfect though they are, have already reached the stage where we can attack the problem with confidence. This does not mean that we can rest on the laurels thus far achieved. Our programs of research must be intensified all over the world. Few investments will pay as large returns. Science must point the way to increased food production, to increased efficiency in food production, to more stable food production, and in addition to find out how all this can be done and still maintain permanently the world's capacity to produce food.

On the average, 90 percent of the world's food is produced in the countries in which it is consumed. That makes it obvious that the task of food production for its people is largely the responsibility of each individual nation. The task can be done more effectively however, if the nations help each other with it. The United States and other countries with highly developed agriculture and industry can be of tremendous help to the under-developed countries in the solution of these problems. I am convinced that if the world of the future is not better fed—that the bottleneck will not be physical resources but ignorance and poverty. The farmers of the world must not only be educated in the use of the more efficient techniques which I have discussed above but they must be supplied with the capital or credit necessary to enable them to take the action which research and education establish as desirable. This world-wide task is not to be accomplished in a few years or even in a generation. It should, however, be far advanced by the end of the present century. It is highly important that each country come to grips with this problem immediately. Long time plans need to be formulated and in many cases, additional research information is necessary before any really intelligent planning can be done. The matter of getting the necessary research done is not simply a matter of appropriating funds. The biggest bottleneck to developments in this field in the next decade will be the shortage of adequately trained personnel. Considering its importance, it is astounding how little attention has been given to this problem in most of the under-developed countries. The number of thoroughly trained soil scientists on the whole of the South American continent can be counted on one's fingers. Hundreds of technically trained agriculturalists will be needed for every one that is available now, if this job is to be well done.

Congress can make millions of dollars available for technical assistance to under-developed countries in a few days but it will take as many years to train enough men to meet the demand. To attempt costly developments hastily and without thoroughly dependable basic information is to court disaster!

FOOTNOTES

1. In "Freedom From Want." A Symposium of the Am. Assn. Adv. Sci. Chronica Botanica. Waltham, Mass. 1948. Pp. 231-3.
2. Ibid. Pp. 253-4.
3. Salter estimates that if these large areas were farmed with the same intensity as similar areas now in cultivation, that the production of most of our major crops could be doubled.

MANAGEMENT OF RESOURCES IN THE TENNESSEE VALLEY

Gordon R. Clapp
Tennessee Valley Authority

Dr. Black has stated facts which emphasize the hope for the future. He also stressed the importance of getting people to put to work the knowledge we have about our resources. Dr. Bradfield has given us facts about the availability of resources to produce food. The primary significance of the TVA in this discussion is that it is a large scale example of management of resources.

During the sixteen years TVA has been at work we have concentrated on three problems, the correction of three basic errors in the organization of the resources of the Tennessee Valley.

The problems and errors are these. First: For many years the productive economy of the Tennessee Valley has wasted the latent energy of the sun and water available in such abundant quantities in that region. This is the region of heaviest rainfall in the United States except the Northwest; a temperate climate with open winters makes possible a long growing season. No other region in the United States has so beneficial a combination of sun and water as the Tennessee Valley, but these resources have been inadequately used due to a cropping system that did not use the soil and water at the most appropriate times of the year. Second: The Tennessee River and its mountain tributaries were not only being wasted as a resource, but were destroying the fruit of man-hours of labor through frequent floods. The third problem can be stated as a consequence of the first two problems: Human energy in the Valley existed in greater quantity than the economy of the region could profitably absorb. The prevailing land-use practices required abundant seasonal labor but did not support the people adequately. There was too little non-agricultural employment.

The TVA has worked with the people of the Valley to get these errors corrected. In the Valley as a whole the devices of management referred to by Dr. Black and knowledge about the resources in the atmosphere and soil referred to by Dr. Bradfield have begun to be applied on tens of thousands of farms. The problem is basically one of management and education — how to get farmers to manage the land in a way that will make it profitable for the farmer to apply practices consonant with good use.

During the ten-year period ending in 1945, out of twelve million acres in the Valley devoted to agriculture, about one million acres have been shifted from row crops to cover crops. Pasture land has been increased by more than 800,000 acres. Rates of application of lime to the soil have increased tremendously compared to areas surrounding the Valley. Similarly, the application of phosphorus materials, essential to make the soil able to grow the crops that capture nitrogen from the air, has greatly increased. There has been a significant increase in the growth of livestock. These practices are evidence and devices of more effective use of sun, soil, water, and the elements in the air, in cycles of productive growth. The practicability of these measures has been demonstrated to the satisfaction of thousands of farmers in the Valley.

TVA has built dams to stabilize the flow of the river and use its energy. At present 27 dams control major floods, provide a navigable channel for commerce, and produce large quantities of electricity. In 1933 the region served by TVA electricity produced and used 1.5 billion kilowatt hours during the year. Today ten times as much (15 billion kilowatt hours per year) is being produced and used. In a few more years the figure will crowd 20 billion kilowatt hours per year. This use of previously wasted energy is bound to have, and already has had, a profound effect upon all economic activity.

The abundance of power has helped to develop opportunities for human energy in non-agricultural pursuits. Since 1933, about 2,100 new industrial developments and manufacturing operations have begun, providing new jobs for about 290,000 people. Of these new enterprises one third are in cities of less than 5,000 people, one third in cities larger than 100,000 people, and the remaining third in cities of intermediate size. The increase in industries in the Valley has been at a rate faster than that for the country as a whole. The same is true for the rate of increase in the number of jobs provided by new industries. This is not surprising in view of the low base from which the development started. Simultaneously there has been a shift of people from rural areas to towns, consequent upon the smaller need for human labor to till the soil and the increased opportunity in non-agricultural occupations.

MANAGEMENT OF RESOURCES IN THE TENNESSEE VALLEY

It is important to remember that with respect to land use in the Valley, we have only begun to achieve the efficient systems the climate, soils and rainfall of the region suggest we should have. With respect to the use of electricity the expansion is far from complete. The point of diminishing returns for the production of electric power has not at all been reached. By no means has the area yet created employment opportunities anywhere near sufficient to keep its human energy occupied. Net out-migration has always been a feature of the Valley's population. The Valley now holds more of its people than it did and provides greater economic opportunity for those who wish to live there. A larger number of people are getting a better living from a better use of the region's resources. And the people are managing their resources in ways that base a greater portion of the Valley's production upon inexhaustible resources and provide more opportunities for human energies in more skilled pursuits.

SOME REFLECTIONS ON WORLD POPULATION AND FOOD SUPPLY DURING THE NEXT FEW DECADES*

Warren S. Thompson
Miami University

I very much fear that the impression which may be left on the general reader by the papers of Drs. Black and Bradfield will be one of easy optimism not only regarding the world's ability to support a rapidly increasing population for a long but indefinite period, but also regarding the ability of each country to do likewise. I do not mean to attribute such a belief to the writers. They have written as scientists and their interest was to present facts regarding the potentialities of agricultural production so that those who are interested in the relation of agriculture and population growth would have the agricultural wherewithal to think clearly about these relations. What I fear is that on the one hand the difference between the potentialities of agricultural production and actual attainment of these potentialities will not be clear to those not familiar with practical agricultural matters and that on the other hand, there will be a tendency to underrate the increase in numbers likely to accompany agricultural improvement in the nonindustrialized areas of the world.

As one who has long been interested in the relation between population growth and the means by which increased numbers can be supported, I have given much study to this matter in its broad aspects. I can also lay some claim to being a practical farmer and to some familiarity with the recent achievements of agricultural science as they affect general farming. Because of this experience I am not disposed to question the views of Drs. Black and Bradfield regarding the possibilities of increased agricultural production. However, I would like to emphasize some of the practical difficulties which stand in the way of applying science to agriculture and to couple these with some observations on the probable increase in population when the application of agricultural science really begins to augment production in nonindustrialized regions.

I have neighbors who have raised as much as 120-130 bushels of hybrid corn per acre against an average of about half that amount for the rest of us. I have yet to find one of them who has done this on as much as 5 acres in any given year although he may have a total of 100 acres or more in corn. Most such yields have been made on only 1 or 2 acres and have seldom been repeated on the same farm. When one asks a farmer with an acre of 125 bushel corn why he doesn't make all his corn acres yield this amount, he looks at you with a pitying smile and asks if you think he is a fool who wants to go bankrupt. To double average yields is at present a <u>stunt</u> and for the individual farmer is a costly stunt. I would make it clear that I am not questioning the possibility of doubling even these <u>stunt</u> yields in years when nature cooperates properly, but I am saying it will not often be done until the price of corn in relation to that of fertilizers and labor and machinery is far higher than it is now. It must be remembered, however, that in any given year a deficiency or an excess of rain, a late spring, and/or an early fall frost resulting in a shorter growing season may have more to do with determining the harvest than the ability of the scientist to produce 3-eared hybrid corn, or a longer head of wheat with extra rows of grains, or beets with higher sugar content.

Furthermore, in the United States at the present time a considerable part of the gain in milk and meat production since hybrid corn came into use is not due to the increased yield of these new varieties, although they constitute a magnificent scientific achievement, but to the fact that instead of producing his own power by feeding his own horses on his own corn, oats and hay he now buys power (gasoline) for his machinery and uses the feed he saves to fatten more cattle and hogs and to keep more and/or better dairy cows.

In my effort to look at the problems of food production in a practical way I do not want to overshoot the mark and belittle the achievements of science. They are great. But I have already lived through three flutters of excitement on the part of the public because of its misunderstanding of the difficulties of translating science into food production, which led many people to believe that lack of food would soon be a thing of the past for all the world. About 30 years ago we were told that chemistry could synthesize all the proteins needed by the human body and that it would be only a matter of a few years until the farmer would no longer have to produce these costly foods—meat, eggs, milk. The chemical industry it was said could provide our proteins so much cheaper than the farmer that the latter could devote all his energy to the production of the carbohydrates which require relatively much less labor. The scientists knew better and cannot be held accountable for this misuse of their facts. But it is significant that one no longer hears any considerable talk of the displacement of farm produced proteins by the chemical industry. For some time yet it appears that the inefficient farmer cooperating with inefficient <u>natural</u> processes can still produce these essentials of diet more cheaply than the factory.

Following on this expected revolution in the production of proteins came the discovery that vegetables, in particular, could be grown with their roots in tanks of water properly impregnated with minerals. An acre of such tanks was to produce the equivalent of many acres of land, and the unit cost was to be far below that of the truck-gardener. The last time I talked to some one familiar with hydroponic production was in Japan where the market for fresh vegetables among the people of the Occupation was lush because the only competition was with imported American vegetables. I was told that the owner of the plant was going out of business although he had the advantage of cheap Japanese labor to operate his plant and could sell his product at American prices. Even under these favorable circumstances the hydroponic gardener could not produce vegetables to compete with the poor quality of imported vegetables which had endured weeks of more or less adequate refrigeration. Hydroponic vegetables like synthetic proteins seem to be passing into the limbo of the forgotten. This is not because a few tanks will not produce as large a tonnage of tomatoes as an acre of land, but because under present conditions a ton of hydroponic tomatoes costs far more than a farmer's ton.

In recent years in the United States we have had much the same excitement over hybrid corn and other improved varieties of grains. At the moment the production of algae as food for yeast which in turn can be used as human food is creating a stir similar to the stir over the synthetic production of proteins 30 years ago. The writer believes that a "wait to see" attitude regarding the replacement of field culture by tank culture is the only sensible attitude for the present.

There are many other scientific achievements through the use of which bigger agricultural production can be attained. Cows which produce more milk and butterfat per unit of feed are being bred; hogs and cattle which add more weight per bushel of corn and per pound of supplement are being grown. Why are the farmers not using them more widely? It is not sufficient to reply with a shrug that they are too conservative. In 15 years I have seen open-pollinated corn entirely supplanted by hybrid and horse-drawn machinery give way to tractor-drawn equipment—a veritable revolution which even a man now only 30 can remember. There is something besides conservatism holding the farmers back. I believe the two chief factors preventing the widespread attempt to grow 125 bushels of hybrid corn, and hogs which will put on weight faster than those now grown are: (a) the lack of the proper organization of farming so that the farmer can fit these new things into his scheme of operation, and (b) the cost of producing these huge crops and of getting the proper breeds of cattle and hogs to convert feed into meat and milk more efficiently. What science can do is one thing; what it is feasible for the farmer to do is often quite another and this is just as true of agriculture in China and India as in the United States.

Regarding the improvement of land Dr. Bradfield has said that it is quite possible to improve greatly the fertility of much land which now produces such poor crops that it does not pay to farm it. I have not the least doubt he is right. As a practical farmer, I have had some experience in doing this. In the process I have doubled my original investment in the land and will never recover it or even get modest interest on it unless farm prices remain near their present levels, or unless other prices are adjusted downward so that the cost of farm production can be reduced. Perhaps my experience is exceptional. There is not the least doubt that much land can be made more productive than it is at present, but I believe that it will be a slow and expensive process absorbing large amounts of capital and labor and often will not pay in any foreseeable future. Like larger crops on land which is already in excellent condition it is not a question of the possibility of increasing the quality of much of our poorer land with our present scientific knowledge of soils, it is a question of practicability— of cost per acre in relation to probable price of product, i.e., of the certainty of return on investment in land in relation to investment in industry and commerce, of the system of land tenure and of other changes which make it feasible to use our science to secure greater and often cheaper agricultural products.

Dr. Black has made the point that it is not the lack of knowledge which holds the productivity of agriculture to its present level, but rather our inability under present conditions to make full use of this science. It seems to me, however, that he has not driven it home as it should be. In the United States just because many improvements in farming are more readily adopted than in most other parts of the world, we are apt to assume that once science makes it possible for labor to become more productive it is only a matter of a few months or years until this greater productivity will be achieved not only here but in all other civilized areas.

RESOURCES FOR THE WORLD'S PEOPLE

It will be altogether impossible even to enumerate the more important obstacles to the adoption of better farm practices in the United States but a further few of them should be mentioned if we are to get a realistic view of what is likely to happen to agricultural production. New or more destructive varieties of old crop pests in the form of insects, plant diseases and weeds are constantly appearing which require increasing attention if larger crops are to be raised. The same is true of the diseases of livestock and often the better bred livestock is more susceptible to these diseases than scrub stock. The use of artificial insemination of cattle which promises rapid improvement in the quality of dairy cattle is by no means a change which can be organized and put into effective practice overnight. In one association I know of personally it has taken about 7 years to get it in fairly satisfactory operation and in the process it has cost some farmers dearly. For beef cattle the practical difficulties even in general farming country have not yet been worked out. Weed control which 2-4-D was assumed to have made readily possible is now said to injure cattle pastured on land so treated and to be especially dangerous for dairy cows since it gets into the milk. The control of flies by the use of DDT is also being found injurious to cattle and many chemists are now saying that no company has a right to market such chemicals until they have been fully tested.

But these more or less technical problems in using better crop varieties and tending them better and in improving livestock are simple compared with the economic and social problems of putting poor land into shape and equipping the farm and the farmer to make use of the latest agricultural science. It seems highly improbable that soil fertility can be built up or maintained under a system of land tenure where more and more of the best land is worked by tenants and where the owner of poor land gets such a small return and hence, remains so poor, that he cannot undertake its improvement. In addition, the social problem of keeping people with adequate training and capital on the land in a civilization where the agriculturist must accept an inferior position, economically and socially, as compared with the industrialist, the merchant, the professional man, and even the handworker in the factory, is a matter to which we have given almost no thought. But it is a vital matter in making good use of science in agriculture.

Finally, revolutionary changes in agriculture just as in industry require changes in organization not only among farmers, but also in the services needed by farmers. Sometimes such changes can be effected rather quickly but at other times they take a considerable period. Changes in the services can be made rather rapidly if sufficient capital is available, but it is not always easy to get the new types of cooperation among farmers that are essential to the successful application of new scientific achievements.

These are only a few of the difficulties that will be encountered in fairly progressive farming areas in making use of a few of the scientific advances in agriculture that have recently become available. Besides, they may not be the most restraining of the difficulties that will be encountered as we are often surprised by the way in which what appear at first minor obstacles become major obstacles. However, we cannot dwell longer on this aspect of the practicability of increasing agricultural production, even in the United States.

There is also one other point which Dr. Black made that I want to emphasize a little more before I enter upon the main point—the relation of population growth to increased agricultural production in nonindustrialized regions. He spoke of the unreality of thinking of world population and world agriculture as though it were a single problem. This is a very important point for, as a matter of fact, the surplus agricultural product of the United States, or Argentina, or Australia, is only available to the people of China or Japan or India if they have something equivalent in value to trade for it. To ignore this simple fact and to speak as though any increase in agricultural production in the United States were available to feed the increase of population in India or some other needy area is wholly unrealistic in the world in which we live. This seems so obvious that it should not need mention. But because of this fact the only really sensible questions regarding the relation of population increase and increase in subsistence must relate to national or, perhaps, regional entities. The conditions that actually prevail or those which can reasonably be expected to prevail in the near future make this necessary.

It is not, then, a question of whether the world can produce food sufficient to care for an additional 10 million or 20 million each year, but whether India can produce enough food, or can trade for enough, to provide for the 5 million or more persons she is likely to have each year subsistence is available until such time as her birth rate is reduced faster than her death rate.

Let me repeat, however, that I do not mean to imply that Drs. Black and Bradfield do not realize the practical difficulties of using our scientific knowledge of agriculture to secure greatly increased production even in the United States to say nothing of those greater difficulties which will be encountered in many other lands. But I fear that many people without their specialized knowledge and practical experience will interpret their statements of what science can do in agriculture as a statement of what is readily and easily feasible among all peoples.

At the present time perhaps 55 percent — 60 percent of the people of the world belong, demographically, in what I have often called Class III, i.e., they have very high birth rates and death rates neither of which is under control although there may be some control over death rates by way of a relatively ineffective public health service. Growth in numbers among these peoples is, as Malthus said, determined very largely by their increase in production — by subsistence. There is a direct relation between the size of the harvest and the growth of population just as there was all over the world until quite recently. Among this 3/5 of the world's people there is very little machine industry and agriculture is carried on in a very primitive and traditional manner and almost entirely by hand labor. Among most of these peoples there are large possibilities for the improvement of agriculture; the probabilities are a different matter. Literacy is so rare among the peasants that it is a very slow and tedious process even to inform them of the possibility of better agricultural practices. These are facts which no one will be disposed to question. In order to indicate probable developments I will try to picture the situation which I believe will arise in these backward industrial lands when their agriculture begins to be more productive. I shall use China and Japan as my chief examples, since I have had some opportunity to observe agriculture in these countries.

In China farms are very small in most regions. Rice is the principal crop, except in the North and Manchuria where millet, kaoliang (a kind of Kaffir corn), wheat, and soybeans are the chief crops and where farms are somewhat larger and more animal power is used. Everywhere, except on a few large estates, farm practices have been fixed by tradition and the peasant is very reluctant to change his practices. Let us suppose that a new variety of rice, or any other crop is developed which will resist disease better, is less subject to attack by insects, does not lodge or shatter as badly as the usual variety, and hence suffers less loss in harvest and, in addition, has a better root system so that it feeds more thriftily. If this new variety could be adopted at once over a wide area, it might add 15-20 percent to the total harvest of that crop. (This is about what is claimed for hybrid corn which is probably the greatest advance made in any one crop in modern times.) As a matter of fact, it will not be adopted all at once as anyone knows. (It took nearly 40 years of hard work to develop hybrid corn before it was ready for the market and even in progressive areas of the corn belt, its adoption was spread over a period of about 15 years.) In China the adoption even of such a variety will certainly be a matter of several decades. The amount of seed available for some years will be small even if the farmer can grow his own seed. If, like hybrid corn, the seed must be grown under carefully supervised conditions and from carefully inbred varieties, then the process will be even slower. It might easily take two generations to bring this improved variety into general use in the area to which it is adapted for we must remember there is no agricultural extension service to convey the knowledge of these improvements to the peasant and the peasant cannot read. He cannot even listen to the radio for most villages have no radio. But if we assume that a 20 percent increase in the yield of an important crop can be achieved in a generation what effect will this have on population?

It is as certain as any thing in human affairs can be that when farmers A and B grow the new rice and get a larger crop and when the other farmers in the village follow their lead the death rate of the village will decline. At first the farmers of this village will also have some surplus to sell, but only after they have eaten more adequately. This more adequate diet will reduce infant and child mortality and what they sell may enable them to repair their wells and to provide mosquito protection and thus to reduce typhoid fever and malaria thereby further lowering their death rate. If agricultural production could be increased 1 percent a year, population growth would consume most of this and at the end of 20 years instead of having 20 percent more to divide among a given number of people the population is more likely to grow by 15 percent or more, leaving very little for use in improving living conditions. The important point to remember is that any general improvement in living conditions will reduce the death rate while the birth rate will be almost unaffected. Indeed, it may increase because the devastating effects of famine and disease will be somewhat mitigated during the period the crop yield is increasing thus ironing out some of the downward fluctuations in the birth rate.

It will be objected that I am assuming an increase in only one crop and that the increase in the yields of other crops might take place simultaneously thus raising the amount of subsistence much more rapidly than assumed here and hence keeping it well ahead of population growth. At this point, I believe the experience of Japan is of much interest.

In the period between 1870 and 1920 (two generations) Japan did increase her food supply by perhaps as much as 80-100 percent while her population increased by about 60 percent. This increase of food supply was achieved both by the extension of the agricultural area (about 40 percent as nearly as I can judge from the figures available), by the improvement of crop varieties, by the intensive use of commercial fertilizer, by better farm practices and by the introduction or extension of the use of crops like potatoes. During this period there was a real improvement in level of living of the people, particularly among those who went to the cities to engage in industry and commerce which were expanding quite rapidly at the same time. Since 1920 yields have not improved greatly and the agricultural specialists of the Occupation speak of a possible increase of 10 percent in staple crops during the next decade but of a much larger increase in potatoes (both Irish and sweet). But this assumes a further large increase in the use of commercial fertilizer, the almost instantaneous spread of potato culture and of the latest scientific improvements in agricultural practice.

What can we learn about China from this Japanese experience? Commercial fertilizer is relatively heavy and bulky and can only be used where fairly cheap transportation is available. In most of China there are no railroads and only a few roads are suited to truck use. It will take some years before the rice farmers of Honan, Human and Szechuan can secure even very modest amounts of commercial fertilizer. In the meantime the increase in yields resulting from the modest amounts they can secure will be consumed largely by the increase in their families due to keeping more of the babies alive. Little will be available to add to capital or to improve permanently their level of living.

It is of great significance also that China has no strong central government which can spread the knowledge of better agricultural practices as could that of Japan, nor can it be assumed that China will develop adequate transportation in the same length of time as Japan, nor that industry will develop fast enough to draw to the cities as large a proportion of the increase of the rural population as it did in Japan. Since 1920, however, Japan's population has increased from about 56 million to 73 million in 1940 and to 81 million at the beginning of 1949 in spite of the war, i.e., by about 30.3 percent between 1920 and 1940 and by almost 11 percent, between 1940 and 1948, or by almost 45 percent in the last 28 years. After 1920 Japan became more and more dependent on outside sources of supply for subsistence. This increasing dependence on outside sources of supply coupled with the increasing difficulties of foreign trade were certainly important factors in the desire of the Japanese militarists and industrialists to secure access to and control over new sources of food supply and larger mineral resources.

I do not believe that anyone who has studied conditions in Japan and China will say that it is reasonable to expect that China can increase her food production as fast as Japan did 1870-1920; nor do I believe it reasonable to expect that China can develop her industry as rapidly as Japan did during the same period, to say nothing of the speed of Japanese industrial expansion 1920-1940.

On the other hand, the social organization of China would lead one to expect that the potential growth of population in China would be greater than that of Japan. I refer particularly to the closely-knit family system of China. Hence, it seems reasonable to believe that population would grow apace with the increase in subsistence even more in China than in Japan. What little is known about birth rates in China also supports this view. They appear to be higher than those of Japan have been within the period when anything is known about them. Certainly the level of living of the Chinese is decidedly lower than that of the Japanese, so much lower that there has been almost no emigration of Japanese into Formosa in those occupations where they had to compete directly with the Chinese. The same is true as regards emigration of the Japanese into both Korea and Manchuria. They went only into the better jobs requiring more education and skill. Furthermore, in the whole area where the Japanese were operating colonies the improvements in agriculture, in transportation, and in public health (small as those in health were), and the incipient development of industry, led to a more rapid increase of the colonial peoples than was taking place in the population of Japan proper. The rates of increase in Korea and Formosa attained the high level of 20-26 per 1,000 per year while before the war Japan itself seldom attained a rate of over 14 per 1,000.

I believe it to be a fact that at present a large part of the world's people — about 3/5 — do increase in numbers almost as fast as their subsistence increases. Furthermore, I believe it to be a fact that the social and economic conditions prevailing in this portion of the world's people precludes a reasonable expectation that they can increase their subsistence, even with the use of our science, at a rate in excess of 2-3 percent a year even under the most favorable conditions for the next two or three generations. Since this rate of increase of production is within the range of possible difference between birth rates and death rates we must look forward to a large increase in this 1.4 billions of people from the time they begin to increase production and to adopt modern sanitary practices until they begin to reduce their birth rates faster than their death rates. Past experience would indicate that this time was at least 5-7 decades in the future. However, it is <u>possible</u> that this period of high natural increase may be reduced for these peoples if they come to appreciate the urgency of their population pressures and are organized to make an active effort to reduce birth rates. It seems to me, therefore, that it requires a hardy optimism, which borders on the uncritical to assume that the application of science to agriculture is likely to remove the pressure of population on subsistence in the near future for the larger part of mankind. It is probably being oversanguine to say that only the 60 percent of mankind referred to above needs worry about subsistence during the next few decades. It seems to the writer that it is also highly unrealistic to assume that the possibilities of agricultural production can be transmuted into actualities within 3-5 decades in much of that additional 20 percent of the world's people which have begun to reduce their birth rates but whose death rates are falling faster than, or fully as fast as, their birth rates.

However, as Dr. Black pointed out there is no sense in asking or trying to answer questions about world population and world food supply; the only questions of significance are those relating to particular peoples and must take into account the actual social and economic conditions in which a people lives. Even those questions suggested below are in many respects too general, but they will indicate the nature of the problems of subsistence and population growth which must be investigated if we are to get any clear notion whether there is a genuine likelihood of any considerable easing of living conditions for the different peoples of the world within the next few decades. Moreover, the answers to such questions should help us to understand better the social, political and economic problems which we must face if we would develop any world organization looking to the improvement of the lot of mankind as a whole.

How fast is it reasonable to expect China and India and other little industrialized countries to develop better yielding varieties of their staple crops, to adopt new crops and to improve methods of tillage? How soon can they be expected to use commercial fertilizer on a large scale and to improve their livestock so that it will contribute largely to an improved level of living? How fast can the customs of land tenure and the organization of the family and the village be changed to make better farming possible? Can the credit structure and other economic institutions be adapted to serve a more progressive agriculture? How fast can we expect these countries to industrialize? Is it reasonable to expect their cities to draw a significant portion of the surplus people from rural communities within 3 to 4 decades, or to expect any decline in the birth rate until such a cityward movement develops on a large scale? Will these backward industrial areas find the conditions of international trade favorable to the export of their raw materials which is the only means by which they can pay for industrial machinery and expert management? With the modern means of communication and the existing knowledge of birth control need it take China and India as long as it did Western lands to reduce their birth rates to the point where population will grow slowly although there is a rapid increase in production? What obstacles does the social system of China place in the way of securing well-trained men, business men, technical men, managers, and experienced machine operators, to operate a modern industrial system? How quickly can these obstacles be removed? With all our great advances in science can the countries which already have dense populations hope to achieve a better level of living as fast as Western Europe did after 1800? What role did the new lands open to European settlement play in the expansion of Europe's population and in the rise in the level of living of European peoples and did it hasten the decline in the birth rate? Can science provide new opportunities to the crowded peoples of Asia which will make up for the lack of new land? Was the relative freedom of trade which prevailed during much of the nineteenth century an important factor in increasing production in the West? If so, can it play the same role in the century to come among the unindustrialized peoples of today?

    The answers to such questions and to many far more specific questions regarding the economy of each country will help us to understand the actual problems of population and subsistence which the different peoples of the world face today. Abstract general questions regarding the relation of population and food are of little value. We must come down to earth and begin to talk about real conditions in given countries if we would appreciate the world's acute population problems.

    Lest I be misunderstood I want to state in unequivocal terms that in my opinion the hope of mankind for a better life lies in his more effective use of science. But man must make wise use of its great achievements if he is not to create as great or greater problems for himself than he had before he began to use them. Unfortunately, very little of our scientific effort has gone into the study of how man may increase his knowledge of his own behavior. Hence, our knowledge of how we may cooperate with <u>natural</u> laws to secure greater control of material things has greatly outdistanced our knowledge of how we may control our own conduct to make better use of our physical knowledge, i.e., how we can use our science to further human welfare by avoiding the unforeseen effects which jeopardize it, of which the too rapid growth of man's numbers is a consequence of the first importance.

I am certain that the men who sought knowledge even when they thought it was "knowledge for knowledge's sake" had vague hopes that this knowledge would contribute substantially to human welfare. Likewise the men who made the practical (engineering) applications of science to agriculture and industry although frequently thinking primarily about the profit to be derived from such use were honestly convinced that their work would add greatly to human welfare and they still are. But because the political, the social, and even the economic consequences of the use of science are frequently more far-reaching than most of us foresee new problems are created by this use which may be almost as serious as those which are solved for the moment. Thus even if we could increase food production for the next few decades twice as fast as appears probable we cannot be at all certain that when the end of such a period arrived most men would be any better off than they now are, unless, in the meantime, we had learned how to control our own conduct as regards the rate of reproduction.

FOOTNOTE

* This paper was written especially for this volume after the conclusion of the annual meeting.

SECTION IV

VALUE SYSTEMS AND HUMAN FERTILITY

Afternoon Session, May 28, 1949
Rudolph Heberle, Louisiana State University, Chairman

THE REPRODUCTIVE MORES OF THE ASIAN PEASANT

Irene B. Taeuber
Princeton University

Cultural continuity and population growth such as have occurred over the millenia in the low-lying plains and river valleys of Asia's southern and eastern littoral imply adjustment between land, technology, fertility and mortality. The most widely accepted explanation of this adjustment is the legacy of a Scotch theologian of the late eighteenth century. It starts with the premise that the ability to reproduce under widely varying conditions is a necessary biological attribute of any species as complicated as homo sapiens, that man did in fact produce in accord with his biological potentialities, that populations grew to the limits of subsistence and were then kept down by the forces of mortality. Doubtless there are places and times in history when this simple thesis explains the dynamics of human survival, but perusal of even the inadequate materials of today's comparative demography reveals the naivete of the arm-chair philosophy and the travelogues that were combined in this broadest of demographic generalizations. There are situations in which abundant breeding creates a population that presses against the absolute limit of physically attainable subsistence—but there are situations where famine, epidemic, and violent death re-enforce the premature mortality of ignorance and malnutrition to make survival impossible, however high the theoretical reproductivity of the human species. Between these two lie a gamut of possibilities, for man does not reproduce to the limit of his biological potentialities, however these may be defined and measured, and mortality cannot be deduced from the abstract facts of climate, land, and food. The vagaries of culture, the ignorance of man, and the menace of insect, bacteria and virus compete with the niggardliness of nature and man's inherent tendency to reproduce as major villains of the demographic saga.

Any dichotomy of fertility and mortality is both factually artificial and analytically sterile if the focus of research is the reproductive behavior of the Asian peasant. Except in transitional periods, the two must stand in

VALUE SYSTEMS AND HUMAN FERTILITY

functional relationship the one to the other. If fertility is inadequate to meet the deaths imposed in the existing situation, the people and the culture disappear. Mortality inadequate to cut survivors to the numbers that can be nourished by the distributed product can be only temporary. The reproductive mores may be regarded as a function of the matrix of factors that determine the timing and the frequency of death, or mortality may be regarded as a function of the effective fertility. In any actual situation reproductive mores and life hazards are interdependent, and both are intermeshed in complicated fashion with the ways of living and of working.

The pursuit of the reproductive balance and the maintenance mores of Asian peasants prior to their contact with the West may seem somewhat esoteric. It is, in fact, deeply tainted with utilitarianism, for all the East is moving away from the necessarily balanced dynamics of peasant societies toward either a reappearance of that balance or the achievement of the more efficient balance made possible by the impact of science and technology on the production and the disappearance of human life. Numerical assessments of the future of Asia's billion peasants abound in both administrative and research literature. They are numerical exercises in which estimates of the present are projected into the future by analogical transfer of the short-time dynamics of other areas. Perhaps this procedure yields valid results, perhaps not. It would seem that the assessment of present and future, whether in terms of projection or policy, of science or problem, could approach technical validity only as it proceeded from analysis of the inherent dynamics of peasant society to the known dynamics of transitional societies and hence ultimately to projection rather than proceeding immediately with a priori manipulations of separable elements whose functional inter-relationships and theoretical limits are unknown.

The statement of this position approaches exercise in theory, for the studies that would permit an empirical approach to the analysis of the reproductive mores of Eastern peasants prior to the impact of the culture of the West have not been undertaken. Demographic analysis of contemporary non-literate people is partial substitute for direct research on a past forever barred from statistical, psychological, and cultural study. There is a fundamental difficulty, however, apart from the fact that ethnologists have failed to make the studies indicated. The non-literate peoples outside the great historic cultures are by definition the groups whose reproductive mores were insufficient to permit a great increase in numbers under the conditions of living and dying that existed

THE REPRODUCTIVE MORES OF THE ASIAN PEASANT

over the millenia when the great human concentrations of the East were developing. Inferences as to the successful in history's demographic race are hazardous if based on the records of the failures. Focused and technically adequate studies within the peasant societies of the contemporary East are essential—but students within and without the area have concentrated either on the reproductive mores of the marginal cultures or on the philosophical and ethnical pronouncements of the great leaders whose words may or may not be related to the beliefs, the values, and the behavior of the illiterate peasant masses. Analysis of available statistics in depth would contribute, but even this remains largely in the stage of discussion and wishful thinking rather than implementation.

The magnitude of the fertility required to insure the survival of Asia's pre-modern peoples may be documented by any one of a series of reasonably plausible manipulations of the contemporary statistics of the peasant East. The preferable illustration is from Japan, for all the historic Japans coexisted in the 'twenties, and all were blanketed by an excellent statistical system. The province of Aomori in far northeastern Honshu represents such a survival in 1925. The outward life of the peasant went on much as it had in the days of the Tokugawa except that children went to school, electric wires crossed the rice paddies, and mortality was substantially controlled. The gross reproduction rate of 3.1 represented the balance of a marriage age substantially beyond puberty and a fertility within marriage little influenced by abortion, infanticide, or contraception. Theoretical maximum fertility would be achieved with this group of women already disciplined to a life of continuing reproduction if marriage occurred at puberty and was ended only by death or widowhood. Under these circumstances the gross reproduction rate would be 4.0, the average number of children borne by a woman surviving the child-bearing period over eight.[1] This fertility, combined with the mortality and the age structure of the life table for British India, 1901-1911, would yield a net reproduction rate of 1.6, a crude birth rate of almost 70. Superficially, this computation may appear to substantiate the traditional thesis that the real demographic problem of the pre-modern period was man's propensity to reproduce in such numbers as to press against the limits of subsistence. There are difficulties, however, for neither the mortality of the India of 1901-1911 nor the hypothetical fertility of the completely married population of Aomori can be accepted as pre-modern patterns. The mortality of the India of 1901-1911 was Western-influenced. Famines and epidemics were limited, the infant and childhood mortality deduced from the registration data of an area in which infanticide had been eliminated. The fertility assumed to be correlated with this artificially lowered mortality yields a crude birth rate unmatched among the peasant peoples of Japan or her former Empire, approached only from the questionable age distributions which were published from the census of Mozambique for 1940. Perhaps total reproductivity of this magnitude once occurred, but it is more in accord with the known facts to assume that there were customs limiting the proportion of the population continuously exposed to the risk of conception, as well as practices designed either to lessen such risks or to eliminate the products of conception through abortion, infanticide, or abandonment. If it is assumed that such limiting factors approached the magnitude that they did in Aomori in 1925, the net reproduction rate is reduced to 1.2, the crude birth rate to 51.2. If we accept this estimate, add to the assumed mortality the actual infant mortality which was probably well above 200 or 225 per 1,000 live births, assume periodically severe malnutrition and a major famine approximately once a generation, permit an occasional epidemic, and introduce some civil disorders and violence, permanent survival becomes precarious.

The recourse to speculative computations based on the contemporary statistics of the peasant East, theoretically so intriguing, has actually led to a morass of conjecture. It does serve to document the thesis that the balance of births and deaths in the pre-modern period was probably precarious, that the basic problem was not the curbing of a super-abundant fertility but the maintenance of the fertility that would insure survival under the hazardous conditions of life that once existed.

Manipulations of the data of today's transitional societies yield no definitive answers as to the demographic balance of the past, but they do serve to destroy the illusion of simplicity and uniformity in that past, to indicate that many demographic adjustments are theoretically possible in any given situation. Moreover, they indicate in striking form the need for concepts and methods other than those developed on the basis of the sophisticated statistical systems of the West. The differences in age structures are so great as to render crude birth and death rates non-interpretable in terms of our own stereotypes of "high" and "low" and thus to remove from our paraphernalia of equipment the ability to evaluate a rate on the basis of its common-sense probability. Furthermore, when neither fertility nor mortality can be assumed to be either stable or regularly changing over time, the measures computed as of a specific period of time refer only to that time period and cannot be inferred to be relevant to the dynamics of the longer period. Perhaps they are; perhaps they are not. Verbal argu-

THE REPRODUCTIVE MORES OF THE ASIAN PEASANT

ment cannot lead to a decision.

Whatever the range of the reproductive performance among Eastern peasants, it is obvious that the lower limits of the fertility that would permit survival were high by today's canons of judgment, and that the reproductive mores of all Eastern cultures had to be oriented toward the maintenance of these high levels of fertility. This is fact, but it contributes little to the analysis of causation or interrelationship and it offers no basis for evaluation of susceptibility or resistance to change and no basis for projection or prediction on other than arbitrary assumptions that are far too likely to represent the emotional state of the projector. It is, furthermore, a fact that does not explain the extraordinary population density generated by the cultures of the East. Peasant economies and high fertility coexist throughout the world. There is no real evidence that the birth rate is higher among the Chinese who till the terraced hillsides of Szechwan, the multitudinous Hindu peasants of the delta of the Ganges, or the clustered Moslem villages of Indonesia than it is among the Bantu whose agriculture of fire and digging stick has hastened erosion and desiccation across the relatively empty lands of east and central Africa. Rice agriculture and irrigation are partial but not sole answers, for they are technically possible elsewhere. The essential aspect of the reproductive mores of the East is not high fertility per se but the inter-penetration of ethical and religious systems, family institutions, social structures, and economic organizations in unified patterns of living that facilitated not merely the production of babies but the preservation of the living. Reproductive mores were not distinct from but integral aspects of the total cultures. It was this fact that gave to the East its great biological strength in history; it is this fact that makes the demographic problems of the present and the future at once so difficult and of such incalculable magnitude.

Ethical and religious values, family institutions, and the replacement of the generations are inseparable strands in the fabric of Asian peasant society. Reproductive and familial mores are the same phenomenon viewed from different perspectives— and both are at once product and cause of the imperatives of the rice agriculture through which Asia's increasing millions secure their sustenance. The goal was not the maximization of pregnancy but the achievement of children who would grow to adult status. Even this was not a goal in any overt sense but rather the unquestioned value of the group, the eternal verity accepted by women, the essential basis for the economic survival of individual, family, community, and ultimately people. The family institution defined the roles of boys and girls in childhood, indoctrinated them concerning the proper relations of the sexes, and specified when and with whom marriage should occur. Sex relations within marriage were presumably socially patterned also, but on this the taboos of the West are so strong that even travelogues avoid the subject. In general, the social compulsions and the correlated individual attitudes insured that most women in the ages in which reproduction was possible bore children with reasonable regularity throughout this span, subject of course to such factors as widowhood and sterility, and cared for the babies they bore according to the procedures traditional in their culture.

The family was critical in group survival or expansion, for from its structure and functioning came the flow of new life and the preservation of the life that existed. But family itself was subject to the compulsions of an economic technology that dictated patterns of labor and thus strongly influenced the relations of the sexes and the status of the generations. The labor of hand agriculture is long and arduous—and the physical production of a long series of babies and the care of those who survive for varying periods of time must occupy the major portion of the time and the energies of women throughout and beyond the reproductive span. Hence it is understandable that in the great cultures, as in most of the nonliterate ones, the heavy labor of the fields became the responsibility of the man. The male role in production and in group participation stood in sharp contrast to the physical dependence of the woman who was occupied by successive pregnancies and continuing child care. Man was pre-eminent, woman subservient. Sons who were potential producers had higher economic value and greater social status than the daughters whose destiny revolved around physical reproduction.

This is a rationalistic and over-simplified explanation of the interrelationships of demographic and economic factors in the generation and maintenance of the great population concentrations of the East. It is not an explanation of cultures in demographic terms, but rather a search for the broadest principles of interpretation under which demographic analysis may be conceptualized. It may be noted that the great value systems of the East have not been considered as separable aspects directly relevant to the analysis of population replacement. More adequate demographic data might invalidate the judgment implicit in this exclusion, but all the data at present available indicate that the great value systems reflect the familial and reproductive mores of the peasant societies from whence they came. Their relevance for demographic process may lie at a deeper level than the con-

THE REPRODUCTIVE MORES OF THE ASIAN PEASANT

tinuing biological maintenance of peasant peoples, for from them may flow the stimuli that lead to the culture of the elite that rises above the peasant base. Expansion in economy and state that permits partial or complete escape from peasantry may be quickened or retarded by the controls, the inhibitions, or the stimulations of ethical and religious value systems. This also is speculative, its validity placed in serious jeopardy by the analysis of the comparative demography of industrialization in Europe and in Japan. In Europe, the Renaissance, the liberation of the intellect, the democratic movement, and the Protestant ethic were presumed to have quickened industrialization and hence its demographic consequences. In Japan all the efforts of the state and the ruling oligarchy were directed toward achieving the power that industrialization gave without paying its social and its demographic costs. Yet the decline in fertility and mortality was quickened in Japan as contrasted to Western Europe.

As the diffusing technologies of the West reached the historic cultures of the East the production available for the sustenance of people was increased and the hazards of life lessened. These technologies reached the East without the intellectual counterparts and the cultural shocks that would have modified basic familial attitudes and altered both the position of women and the role of children. Early marriage and socially sanctioned childbearing remained. The many sons who had been an unrealizable ideal for the masses in the pre-modern period now became both realizable and profitable, for to the individual peasant the increase of his own labor force meant enhanced production and greater security in old age. Behavior developed over the millenia as the essential basis for individual and group survival now produced an abundance of children that menaced survival at the more humane levels made possible by order, medical and sanitary technologies, and improved agriculture.

The common assumption is that the reproductive mores of the peasant East are highly resistant to change. That they are resistant is beyond dispute, but the use of the adjective is debatable. The reproductive mores of the majority of Europe's peasants were transformed only over the course of the centuries. Moreover, the reproductive mores of Asia's peasants have yielded, just as did those of the West. In Japan the process of demographic transformation was quickened as compared to that of European cultures as a whole, although case histories are as yet too limited for definitive East-West comparisons. There is accumulating evidence that fertility yields under the stimulus and the pressures of modernization, whether the group concerned be the Catholics or the Prot-

VALUE SYSTEMS AND HUMAN FERTILITY

estants of the West, the Confucians of China, the Buddhists of Siam, the Shintoist of Japan, or the Moslems of Indonesia. Perhaps changing economies and changing class structures alone are involved; perhaps the intensity of the ancient values and the resistance to the acceptance of the new differ from group to group as between cultures or as within individual cultures. The resistances that exist, moreover, may be of quite different types. The verbalizations of the elite lead to the inference that the reproductive and the familial values of the peasant East are highly rationalized and firmly entrenched. Discussions with those who know the peasants of this same East substantiate the thesis that the reproductive mores are accepted as natural, unquestioned because they have always been and nothing else is envisioned as possible. Both these interpretations assume unquestioned acceptance of traditional values, yet literature documents the tensions of the upper groups, while the ever-recurrent problem of infanticide documents the tensions of the peasant masses and the urban workers. Together these offer incontrovertible evidence of the existence of severe strains even prior to contact with the apparently irresistible social forces generated by Western expansion.

Fertility has become super-abundant again and again in the past, for the unchanging East is itself a myth. The present is only the longest of a series of maladjustments, the one most devastating in its human consequences if it is to end with the restoration of the pre-existing balances. Whether it will do so or not is still conjectural. The answer lies in part in political factors, in part in the nature and rapidity of the economic developments, but at least equally in the rapidity with which the reproductive mores of the peasants yield. There is abundant quantitative evidence that they will yield. The question is not the fact of transformation but the rapidity. The human welfare of half of all mankind depends on the answer. And the research basis for that answer can be found only in field studies of the reproductive mores, their nature, their intensity, and their differential susceptibility to change.

FOOTNOTE

1 Actual assumption, 95 per cent marriage by age 15. Fertility of this magnitude has been recorded in the transitional society of Korea. With the Korean life table of 1925-1930 and the age distribution implicit in that mortality, the gross reproduction rate 4.0 by definition, the net reproduction rate becomes 1.9, the crude birth rate 56. Neither birth rates nor rates of natural increase of this magnitude have characterized Japanese developments in the late feudal or the early post-restoration period.

DEMOGRAPHIC VALUES IN THE MIDDLE AGES*

Josiah C. Russell
University of New Mexico

During the Middle Ages there were usually two sets of demographic values in circulation, one presented by the Church and the other the customary standards of the laity. The Church as an institution was everywhere, had a definite opinion about many phases of life and exerted a constant and powerful influence through the pulpit and the confessional. The evidence of its beliefs as they pertained to demography appears in systematic treatises upon theology and in manuals for confessors. The opinions of the laity are not so easy to gather since they must be derived for the most part from the practices of the people themselves.[1] To make clear the nature of the two sets of values we may say that the clerical values were based upon the supreme worth of the human soul and the lay set upon the superior value of human dignity. To a remarkable extent the two sets of values were similar; the divergence is evident in only a few particulars.

The soul was considered the province of the Church while human dignity was a matter for the individual. Both of these were thus superior to either the family or the state in the estimation of the people. The type of allegiance involved in these points of view had definite results in demographic trends of the time, upon birth and death and even upon migration and social mobility. We shall consider the forms of allegiance in order as they relate to Church, individual, family and state.

The superior allegiance of the clergy to the Church is indicated best by the enforcement of celibacy upon the clergy. It is doubtful if the majority of the mediaeval clergy was ever very enthusiastic about celibacy; it was first enforced on them by the laity who believed that saints and bishops should be celibate and then by the older and higher clergy who had been accustomed to it and regarded it as very valuable for the soul. Whatever the reason, celibacy produced a terrible intellectual and social loss in the Middle Ages. The homes of the clergy must have numbered at least half of the prosperous homes of the period and, of course, a much greater proportion of the educated homes. The loss of these homes as families raising children was a great source of weakness to the society of the time and especially to the Church itself. One has only to consider the great number of children coming from the homes of the Protestant clergy today to realize the Church's loss. In fact the decline of the clergy in the late Middle Ages is probably due more to celibacy than to any other single cause.

As against celibacy which tended to reduce at least one type of population, other Church teachings tended rather to increase population.[2] The human soul was considered alive and inviolable at conception. Thus, once started, the soul, by Church doctrine, was entitled to life and might be disturbed or destroyed only by commission of mortal sin. Moreover, theologians were inclined to approve of the Biblical injunction to increase and multiply. It can be seen then that, given these ideas alone, there would be no real check upon populations increasing.

The laity of the Middle Ages were largely agricultural and visual minded. The lay demographic ideal then was essentially that of the mediaeval village. In each village there were usually a certain number of holdings of similar character which required the efforts of a mature male, physically and mentally; about thirty acres of land together with a quota of animals upon the manor. In addition there were lesser holdings which did not require so much effort. The situation was usually static except that with better farming additional land might be added, but little of this occurred since it must be subtracted from woodland and pasture which were already essential for the manorial economy. The ideal of the established holdings appears again among the gilds of the cities.

Obviously only the full holdings could be expected to care for a family satisfactorily in the eyes of the lay population. Thus naturally marriage would be restricted to those who had holdings: these were acquired by inheritance, by marriage, and sometimes by gift or purchase. The principle of no holding, no marriage, operated as a fairly effective check upon population increase. The conditions of mortality tended to make the average age of marriage for the young men vary between twenty-two and twenty-five years. It also meant that the weak in mind or body were not permitted to marry and thus mediaeval society gained by whatever advantage such a restriction offered.

Since population varies from family to family, village to village and generation to generation surpluses turned up from time to time which

DEMOGRAPHIC VALUES IN THE MIDDLE AGES

created problems for the mediaeval laity which was keenly interested, as we have said in preserving satisfactory subsistence. These problems appeared most prominently at birth and marriage. The ecclesiastical doctrine denied that anything could be done at birth to prevent overpopulation. The lay ideal was quite different, as is clear from the evident excess of males over females in the population. Only a definite tampering with life after birth could have produced the difference in number of the sexes. The lay ideal then very definitely operated to keep population within the limits which seemed necessary to preserve adequate subsistence for society.

Control, based upon relating of marriage to jobs, might have increased population if the jobs were multiplied greatly. This could have been accomplished in the Middle Ages if the industrial revolution had occurred then rather than in the 18th century. To do this the mediaeval gilds would have had to accept the machine and inventions. However, they apparently regarded machines as unfair advantages for a few which would have lost jobs for the great majority. Parliament even outlawed them in England. Thus again the opportunity to increase population was lost.

The second place where surplus population could be controlled was at marriage — the surplus included two classes, the physically and mentally normal and the physically and mentally weak. The two types presented different problems which were settled within the lines laid down by mediaeval respect for the individual.

Local surplus of landed population (the one large increasing group) was cared for by migration and social mobility.

Migration from one manor to another was facilitated by sale of serfs or by permission to leave the manor. The migrant might retain his rights of hereditary succession in the manor by appearing in the manor court at one or two stated times a year and paying a nominal sum of money, usually called a head tax.

Much migration, which also involved social mobility, moved from country to city, as farmers became freemen of the cities. Similarly by the payment of a small sum the serf could enter the clergy. Because the Church officials reproduced but slightly and the city failed to replenish its own population there was little migration in reverse direction. Social mobility was sufficient to prevent the establishment of a caste system.

The problem of the surplus at marriage which was feeble physically or mentally could hardly be settled either by migration or mobility. Nor in view of the ecclesiastical opinion of the sanctity of the soul and the lay ideal of the dignity of the individual would the frequent solution of either the primitive or the Nazi be used—death. The mediaeval solution was a happy one—the feeble were settled as cottars in their own cottages, supported by a few acres of their own, by reservation of part of the produce from the family land, by gleaning in the fields after the harvest, and by paid labor in the village. Simple tasks such as herding were often assigned to them. The result was a dignified solution of the social security problems.

Already we can see that the family was not an end in itself. There was no attempt to maintain a family by means which modern Oriental societies use; early marriage and the piling up of families under one roof. Mediaeval society believed in no ancestor-worship and thus avoided the serious overpopulation of ancestor-worshipping societies.

The family was subordinate to Church and individual but it was, nevertheless, a very good economic unit, a part of the larger and also excellent unit, the manor. Every member of the family, given any strength or intellect, contributed to the family support and shared in the family prosperity.

When Adam and Eve span little Boy Blue was out in fields and should have been watching the flocks. Thus the mediaeval family attained a notable adjustment amid the environment of its day. Finally there is the state to be considered. Unlike the modern nation the mediaeval state made no extreme demands upon the citizen. Indeed, no concept of the powerful state existed. Revolt against the state by feudal lords was a frequent occurrence and seldom drew the death penalty.

In fact although death was supposed to be punishment for many crimes criminals frequently escaped, either by flight before capture, by outlawry, or by reaching sanctuary in any of the numerous churches which had that right.

Great areas of jurisdiction were held by the Church outside of the control of the state. No clerk might be tried before the lay courts, and since canon law did not prescribe the death penalty, the clerks were exempt.

The state then exerted no influence, as it has in certain countries in our time, to increase the population for purposes of national prestige or military power.

This then is the picture of the demographic values of the Middle Ages and of their effects upon population. They produced, by their emphasis upon the value of the human soul and the dignity of the individual, a remarkably stable, if slowly increasing population. Clerical celibacy prevented the appearance of the literate family and the antagonism to the machine postponed the Industrial Revolution; only modern times have seen these developments. By and large the mediaeval period was remarkable for the high ideals which were set up for both the great and the small people, for the feeling that success belongs to the pure in soul as well as the rich and the powerful. These very great contributions to western civilization were tied in very closely to the demographic values of the time.

FOOTNOTES

* More detailed discussion of this subject may be found in the author's British Mediaeval Population (Albuquerque, 1948), chapters VII and XIII, and in his yet to be published Mediaeval European Population.

1. In this study we omit the effect of the decline and rise of population during the first and last parts of the Middle Ages and the conditioning of persons as a result of these changes.

2. It may be debated whether the sanctity of marriage retarded or encouraged population increase. Retarding would occur as illegitimacy was discouraged and illegitimate children discriminated against. Increasing would be encouraged with clerical insistence that no birth control be attempted.

THE CATHOLIC VALUE SYSTEM IN RELATION TO HUMAN FERTILITY

Rev. William J. Gibbons, S.J.
National Catholic Rural Life Conference

In a philosophy of life which accords with Catholic thinking, human fertility is not a factor to be isolated from other values. If for purposes of scientific study we consider it apart, this is presumably with the remembrance that man is a unity whose various functions and capacities are ordered by nature to a single end— achievement of beatitude in the life to come. Such is the philosophical and ethical premise from which the Catholic proceeds in his study of fertility. It is a premise shared in substance, if not in every conclusion deducible from it, by all who affirm a rational basis for human conduct. That includes many ethicians of all ages, non-Christian as well as Christian. Such an approach is at once alien to sentimental, positivistic, materialistic interpretations of human behavior.

When making value judgements and determining conduct norms about human reproduction, the Catholic moral thinker emphasizes especially the rational. He knows that nowhere more than in the area of sex is it easier to obscure the reasoning process through undue attention to passion and emotion. Nevertheless in reaching specific conclusions as to the propriety of given conduct, he does not confine himself to deductive reasonings about man's nature, but also takes into account human behavior in a concrete environment. This is not to say that the Catholic ethician or moralist draws rules of behavior from what *is*, but rather that in principle if not always in practice, he takes into consideration the findings of the natural and social sciences when determining what *ought* to be.

Sound Catholic thought recognizes that if moral science has its own terms of reference and formal object, so too do the social sciences in their various ramifications. No good purpose is served when the moralist oversteps the bounds of his science and draws inferences as to what *is* from his own conclusions about man's moral obligations in the abstract. Neither is the cause of truth advanced when the student of the social sciences departs

THE CATHOLIC VALUE SYSTEM IN RELATION TO HUMAN FERTILITY

from his field of investigations to lay down rules of conduct based primarily or exclusively upon what some men do or wish to do.[1]

By keeping in mind the delimitations of their respective sciences, the moralist and social scientist can get along together. Furthermore, inasmuch as the subject of their study is the same, namely man, they can cooperate in aiding modern men to adapt themselves to their environment, and also modify it in such a way that man's purpose on earth is more readily achieved.

If such mutual understanding and cooperation is objectively possible, how does it come to pass that in certain conclusions concerning the complex of values surrounding human reproduction, the practicing Catholic on occasion finds himself at odds with many manifestly sincere persons who also base their ethical behavior upon a rational foundation? A partial answer may be drawn from what was already said concerning occasional confusions about the limits of the moral and social sciences. But the major explanation for the disagreement, it would appear, must be sought in the Catholic concept of the Church's teaching authority. That authority is not taken as a denial of reason but as its complement and safeguard. The Catholic moralist and social philosopher each approaches his field with the conviction that the Church, by reason of the divine guidance accorded it, is in a position to make definitive decisions regarding questions of human values and moral conduct. These decisions are not arbitrary. Nor are they mere practical norms of behavior consequent to current ecclesiastical policy as it adjusts itself to the contemporary scene. Rather, definitive pronouncements on disputed moral points are conceived as the necessary and supernaturally provided adjuncts to the rules of ethical conduct derived from reason.[2]

Acceptance of these definitive rules, which are at times admittedly irksome to man, is regarded by the Catholic Church as obligatory in conscience, just as much as are the primary dictates of the natural law imprinted on the minds of men. This conclusion derives in turn from the belief that Christ, the Divine Teacher, not only laid down certain explicit rules of conduct Himself, but also left behind a permanent teaching body which would be safeguarded from error when removing authoritatively doubts on specific points of human behavior.[3] Sometimes these moral imperatives accepted by the Catholic conscience are quite explicit. At other times they are clearly deducible from some other definitive pronouncement on doctrine or morals.

Failure to distinguish clearly between the absolute norms of conduct authoritatively laid down, and the adaptable disciplinary rules of the Church is responsible at times for a feeling among those not of the Catholic faith, that sooner or later some adjustment will be made on basic teaching regarding sex, marriage and the family. The fact is that while fuller implications behind certain doctrinal truths are constantly being discovered, the essentials of Catholic belief remain unchanged. The Church never reverses herself on authoritative moral definitions any more than she does in the case of doctrine. Individual members do indeed fall short of the ideal, and even cease practicing their religion, but the teaching Church does not therefore modify the body of truth she is assigned to guard.

This, be it noted, is a reasoned position springing from the firm conviction that the Church's authority is not of human origin. Hence the Church, in making moral pronouncements, is not authoritarian, much less totalitarian, in the manner that man-made governments are when they usurp unwarranted authority over the consciences of men.[4] There is a higher law to which even the supreme rulers of the Church must themselves submit. Human beings take justifiable pride in subjecting their conduct to reason, especially in the face of conflicting emotions. In the same light, the Catholic regards his own submission to the teaching Church in its authoritative pronouncements, even though the non-rational part of his nature prompts otherwise. He believes that the pope or a universal council does not make truth, much less modify it at will, but merely clarifies what already is true.

I. <u>The Rational Use of Sex</u>. To return more specifically to the position of the Church on human fertility. Man, though composed of body and soul and endowed with a multiplicity of capacities, is a unity. With the animals he shares sense faculties and impulses. Unlike the animals, he is also possessed of a spiritual soul, created by God for eternal existence in heaven. Rational by nature, this composite creature man is capable of regulating his impulses and instincts according to the rules of an objective order, of which his reason becomes progressively aware. He does not create this order out of his mind, which is, unfortunately, at times beclouded by emotion and confused or prejudiced in its approach to moral truth.

Rather, man in studying the universe about him and in sounding the inner mysteries of his own person, comes to see that God the Creator has endowed man with a nature which must find its perfection in a particular way. This it does through the exercise of intelligence and within the framework of an objective scheme of things which transcends the whim and desire of the individual person. Man the reasoning animal, recognizes that he has no logical alternative but to embrace and follow the rules of conduct which his nature and the order of creation dictate. To do otherwise, as well he may because of the freedom of choice wherewith he is endowed, is to distort the role assigned him and to risk his eternal salvation. Accordingly, strictly human acts, as distinguished from involuntary responses on the sense level, are always in the concrete moral or immoral. Without morality, man would not be man.[5]

To cite enlightened reason as the guiding norm of moral conduct, is not to deny that the sense and rational levels of man's being can, at any given moment, be oriented in different directions. But in the event of conflict, reason is supposed to win out. Obedience to the rule of reason and to an enlightened conscience, may sometimes occasion suffering, even death itself. But sacrifice is integral to man's existence in this world. The need for such sacrifice, men are accustomed to recognize in many departments of life, not excluding the duty of surrendering one's life in defense of the fatherland. There is no law of personal development or of self-expression which negates the moral law, with its individual and social responsibilities. Self-conquest, discipline, the practice of moral restraint are, in the nature of things, the concomitants of a moral life. Nowhere is this more true than in the ordering of sex, a dominant passion of the average man.[6]

Now, it is perfectly obvious to anyone who understands the physiology of the sexual organs of man, and the psychic reactions connected with them, that these are by nature ordered to one end, namely human reproduction. The fact that the urge to use these faculties is more or less persistent in the normal person in no way leads to the conclusion that their use can go unregulated by reason. Self-restraint may be difficult, but it is not impossible. The reproductive urge is, of course, so strong in the human race that in the normal course of events the vast majority of men marry. Thus the human species is continued, and the divine directive, "Increase and multiply," is carried out.

Such a development leaves room for a number of individuals to renounce marriage and the legitimate satisfaction of the reproductive urge. The duty to reproduce is incumbent upon the race; not upon every single individual in it. Even though some individuals avail themselves of their freedom not to marry, they can do so with good conscience knowing that relatively few will follow their example. Accordingly, perpetual continence is morally permissible, and may for specific individuals be the better course, when embraced for a good motive or through necessity, without danger of unchastity. Perfect chastity, or virginity, Christian tradition teaches, is in itself preferable to marriage, when chosen for supernatural reasons.[7]

VALUE SYSTEMS AND HUMAN FERTILITY

Even in marriage itself, temporary continence for spiritual reasons of penance, self-restraint or dedication to a higher work, is legitimate and praiseworthy, provided the rights of neither party are disregarded. Moreover, in Catholic annals there are recorded marriages of saintly persons who observed perpetual continence by mutual agreement. Whether in all cases this was praiseworthy objectively, might indeed by questioned, particularly where offspring were desirable because of serious social considerations.

Attention is called here to the moral legitimacy of such continence, to forestall any suspicion that in the case of married persons Catholicism correlates sanctity with the number of children born. At times confusion arises in the minds of some regarding this point, so that the Catholic moral and ascetical tradition may be in part overlooked. Vermeersch, the moralist, after laying down some general rules as to the use of marriage, sums up the traditional attitude thus, "For the rest, the use of marriage is not directly prescribed for the spouses by any law."[8]

The reproductive function in man is directed toward the family, which is the only institution adapted to the proper care and education of children brought into the world by reason of human fertility. With most of mankind, Catholicism regards the family as the basic unit of society, whose sanctity must be respected under penalty of grave social ills. The begetting and rearing of children is one of the most responsible tasks man could undertake. It is also a sacred task, for not only are the parents cooperating with God in the production of human life; they are also the occasion of God's creating another soul destined for eternal life.[9]

Abuse of sex in any manner whatsoever is considered within the Catholic framework of values, as sinful, an offense against the law of nature and of God. The pleasures associated with the use of sex are, as it were, a stimulus and a reward for willingness to accept the responsibilities which are the consequent of human reproduction. To voluntarily seek or accept such pleasures in a manner which excludes the primary end of marriage, namely reproduction, is seriously sinful and places man in an inimical relationship to God so long as he remains in an unrepentant state. Catholic moral thinking says in effect, that just as man may not violate the law of self-preservation by wilfully destroying his health or life, so neither may he make arbitrary use of the reproductive capacity God has given him.

This emphasis upon the primary end of marriage, and upon the relationship of sexual activity to reproduction, is not intended as a denial of other legitimate ends of marriage. Mutual aid and the quieting of concu-

THE CATHOLIC VALUE SYSTEM IN RELATION TO HUMAN FERTILITY

piscence, to use the traditional terminology, are recognized objectives of married life. These secondary purposes are in fact predominant in the minds of most persons entering upon marriage. Such an orientation need not conflict with sound ethical norms, so long as it implies no positive exclusion of the fundamental reason for marriage as an institution.

Those persons who, throughout the centuries, have regarded marital intercourse for motives other than reproduction as something unlawful, or at least improper, inadequately understand the nature of marriage. The fostering of mutual love, the rendering of the marriage debt, the avoidance of unchastity, are reasonable motives for intercourse and for cohabitation under a common roof. What Catholic moral teaching objects to is not these elements of mutuality or the expression of love and personality, but rather the subversion of the ends of marriage in such wise that the secondary ends become primary, and the primary end is denied in principle or positively excluded in practice.

As a value system, Catholicism endeavors to impress upon men the truth that perfect happiness comes only with the attainment of eternal salvation. Man's temporal life is a testing ground, wherein success is determined on the basis of the individual's readiness to conform to the divine plan. This plan does not forbid what is good for man, but only puts moral restraint upon him to avoid what runs contrary to his nature and destiny. By stressing these truths, Catholic teaching proves itself the convinced defender of human liberty and the opponent of any effort to reduce the human person to the non-rational level, on which impulse would be the internal driving power, and physical force the only ultimate means of external control.

That the mastery of sex is difficult, Catholic teaching fully recognizes. Approaching the matter theologically, it can be said that had Adam and Eve, the first human pair, been obedient to God, they and their children would have continued in the state of original justice. That state, characteristically identified with the possession of the supernatural gift of sanctifying grace, also carried with it certain other gifts, among which integrity is always listed by the theologians. Put briefly, possessed of integrity in the theological sense, man would have been able to regulate his passions, without the conflict of tendencies now experienced. Unclouded reason would have ruled, so that present difficulties in keeping the use of sex on a rational level could have been avoided. God in redeeming fallen man, did not see fit to restore the gift of integrity. But He did assure sufficient grace necessary to keep the moral law; it is up to man to accept it. Difficult as is the observance of chastity, even at times within the married state, it is not beyond man's capacities, provided he avails himself of the sources of grace God has opened up to him.[10]

II. <u>Chastity, Safeguard of the Family</u>. In the hierarchy of values accepted by the Catholic Church, chastity is regarded as the safeguard of the family. Jacques Leclercq, the French Catholic ethician, has ably summed up the relationship between chastity, continence and married life. He writes, "We speak of chastity and continence. Chastity is the virtue whereby a person brings and keeps the sex instinct under the control of reason. Continence implies chastity, but chastity can exist without continence. In married life, conjugal chastity calls at times for continence and at times merely for moderation."[11] Thus Leclercq draws attention to the now evident sociological fact, that men will progressively lose esteem for sound family life when they have no hesitation in gratifying sexual impulses apart from marriage. Also implied is the further truth, recognized by many psychiatrists and sociologists, that the conceiving of marriage solely as an opportunity for sexual gratification cuts the very foundation from beneath family stability.

Prior to marriage, youth are morally bound to chastity and continence, which not a few, aided by grace accept with a high degree of spiritual motivation. Nor is this period of pre-marital chastity a bad thing, even from the psychological and sociological viewpoint. Early marriages are not the unmixed blessing their advocates sometimes make them out to be, nor are they any substitute for the disciplined practice of chastity in youth. Man is made in such a way that the reproductive capacity and urge are present before the emotional and intellectual maturity desirable for responsible family life has been arrived at.[12] If the voluntary acceptance of perfect and perpetual chastity for spiritual reasons implies a degree of virtue of relatively rare occurrence, it does not therefore follow that the observance of chaste continence when circumstances require it, is beyond man's moral capacities or harmful to him physically and psychologically.

Catholic thought recognizes that the number of the willingly celibate is augmented by many individuals who for reasons beyond their control, are not in a position to find a legitimate outlet for the sexual urge. That such "victim cases" must be prepared for sacrifice is admitted. But sacrifice of some sort is the lot of all men at one time or another in the carrying out of moral duty. The self-restraint these individuals have to practice can be turned by them to their own moral and spiritual advantage.

While on the subject of self-restraint, which at times implies some degree of continence, it is desirable to clarify a point which occasions some

THE CATHOLIC VALUE SYSTEM IN RELATION TO HUMAN FERTILITY

misunderstanding. The primary end of marriage is the begetting of children.[13] That is the reason for the generative organs in man, and the moral justification of marriage as a state of life. Nevertheless, Catholic teaching properly understood, does not encourage the exercise of the reproductive function in marriage without any regard for how the children born will be brought up. Fully aware of how readily many persons would turn to illegitimate sexual gratification were too many obstacles placed in the way, the Church has always shown herself more disposed to encourage marriage than to set up barriers. But this does not mean she approves imprudent fertility. Catholicism would be going against the basic ethical principle of subjecting passion to reason, were it to praise, for example, the shortsighted abandon of those who regard marriage as a legitimized opportunity for unrestrained sexual gratification.[14] Unfortunately the careless language of some popular writers at times conveys the wrong impression. Both chastity and continence have their place, even within the married state. Nor is the practice of the two unconnected psychologically.

If Christian principles urge chastity and restraint, and hold up virginity as an ideal, that implies no condemnation of marriage. God's creation of a helpmate for Adam, and His treatment of the first human pair indicate differently. In the New Testament, Christ raised marriage to the dignity of a sacrament. Thus is the marriage contract of the baptized blessed and made a medium of grace, both at the time of the marriage and in the difficult years that follow.

The sacramental character of marriage is not intended as a cloak for something evil. Catholic belief does not regard concupiscence as sinful, unless occasioned or yielded to sinfully. Nor does it conceive of intercourse and fertility as sinful. Not the use of marriage but its abuse is wrong. Hence, the married state is in itself something good, and the normal vocation for the vast majority of men. It is, however, important that in entering into marriage man recognize the true character of the contract. Nor man, but God has made the rules which govern it.[15] Adherence to these rules, which is impossible without the practice of chastity, is the safeguard of marriage as an institution.

III. <u>Some Specific Means of Regulating Fertility</u>. Before discussing Catholic thinking on human fertility in relation to world population trends, it is desirable to clarify the Church's position on several points which sometimes occasion misunderstanding. The Catholic value system, not only as related to marriage but also to human personality, includes very definite attitudes toward sterilization and birth control.

Direct sterilization, whether for eugenic or simple birth control purposes, is clearly outside the moral pale so far as Catholics are concerned. This does not imply a desire to see individuals who lack aptitude or discretion, bring children into the world without regard for ability to care for them. Among the moral imperatives Catholicism enunciates, is that the welfare of the children must be taken into consideration when making use of marriage. But if individuals entering marriage have a heavy moral responsibility in this regard, it still remains true that the physical as well as the spiritual integrity of the human person must be held sacred. The Catholic Church conceives of direct sterilization as an unwarranted attack upon the dignity of the human person.[16] It is in this light that the question of sterilization should be reviewed.

Catholic thinking has always recognized the lawfulness of surgical operations which might deprive the individual of some organ or limb, but which are necessary for preservation of life or proper health. Consequently, there has been no serious question among Catholic moralists about the legitimacy of operations which might result indirectly in sterilization. In specific cases, moralists may question the legitimacy of given techniques because there is doubt about the necessity of the operation or the intention of surgeon or patient. Doctors as a rule tend to play safe, and on occasion go beyond the limits of their science by counselling operations of this sort primarily to avoid what they at times refer to as "complicating pregnancies." Moralists, on the other hand, insist rightly that in a matter of such moment as preserving the integrity of the generative organs, need for an operation resulting in sterility should not be assumed lightly. However, in the present discussion it is neither possible nor necessary to examine in detail the delicate questions of medical ethics.

The problem before us is not indirect sterilization, but rather what is referred to as <u>direct</u>. In times past this was often referred to as eugenic sterilization and was advocated for purposes of preventing reproduction by the mentally deficient or the criminally insane. Not infrequently advocates of this sort of sterilization, in urging that it be sanctioned legally and practiced on governmental authority, proved overzealous in their cause. They put forward exaggerated claims as to the extent of mental deficiency and at times even made themselves ridiculous by confusing the respective roles of heredity and environment. But there have been other advocates of sterilization who recognized the danger inherent in having so much power over the human person in the hands of public officials, and sought to safeguard

THE CATHOLIC VALUE SYSTEM IN RELATION TO HUMAN FERTILITY

the individual by elaborate legislative precautions. In <u>Population Roads to Peace and War</u>, Guy Irving Burch and Elmer Pendell have given us a summary on the state of sterilization legislation throughout the world.[17]

It would be unfair to call into question the sincerity of the proponents of legal sterilization. Many, no doubt, had and still have the interests of society at heart. What they tend to overlook, however, is the essentially moral nature of the question. Not every means of solving social problems is necessarily legitimate, nor even socially desirable. The full range of human and social values must always be taken into consideration. We are faced again in this instance with the necessity of avoiding an isolated approach to sex or the reproductive function.

Speaking sociologically, widespread recourse to direct sterilization would endanger the individual's right to bodily integrity. It might easily lead to conflicting policies in regard to population, which would resemble too closely those of the Nazis. The German National Socialists presented the spectacle of encouraging sterilization of the so-called unfit while at the same time making quite acceptable the practice of childbearing outside of wedlock. Similar contradictions in social theory can usually be found among those who make a biological rather than a moral approach to the question of human fertility. Social consideration must never be overlooked, least of all by the moralist, but when conflict occurs, Catholic social philosophy insists what is socially expedient must be determined within the framework of definite moral principles.

Thomas Aquinas summarized the generic argument against mutilation. Moralists subsequently applied the principle to questions of direct sterilization. At times, however, doubts arose in the minds of some as to the power of the state over the bodies of the criminal or unfit. Pope Pius XI made a clear pronouncement on so-called eugenic sterilization in the encyclical <u>Casti Connubii</u>. Catholic thought on the subject crystalized.

All possible doubt was removed in a decree of the Holy Office in 1940. The Holy Office, the department of the Vatican with jurisdiction in such matters, was asked: "Whether the direct sterilization of man or woman, whether perpetual or temporary, is licit." The reply was precise "In the negative; it is forbidden by the law of nature, and, as regards eugenic sterilization, it is already condemned by the Decree of this Sacred Congregation, of 21 March, 1931. Approved, confirmed, and ordered to be published by His Holiness, Pius XII in the audience of 22 February, 1940."[18]

In seeking, therefore, a solution of problems of economic hardship, population pressure or eugenics, Catholics do not think in terms of sterilization. This does not mean that Catholic social thought overlooks the existence of these problems, but rather that it circumscribes the area in which morally acceptable remedies may be sought. Before taking up, however, a discussion of the Catholic position on such questions, it is desirable to say something about birth control in relation to human fertility.

The traditional attitude of the Church toward fertility and the birthrate is primarily a positive and constructive one. In line with Christian teaching, children are welcomed because they are new souls destined for eternal life. Leclercq in his <u>Marriage and the Family</u>, puts it thus, "To bring a child into the world under conditions favorable to his development as a human being is one of the greatest works that man can perform. It constitutes the glory of marriage."[19]

Considered in itself, fertility is a blessing, signifying not only the obedience of the race to God's command to increase and multiply, but also the extension of the individual and family's own being. The blessing of a fertility conformable to reason is so great, that had mankind remained in its original state of innocence, from which the vice of lust was excluded, virginity and continence would not have been praiseworthy. Their particular virtue in the fallen state of nature derives from the fact that they bring passion under the control of reason, and thus assist the mind to attend to higher things.[20]

But human fertility, since man is a creature of reason and not mere instinct, must be a reasonable fertility. Multiplication of children as a result of license, or over-indulgence, or improvidence, implies varying degrees of moral guilt, depending on the extent to which the individual is personally responsible, and the relationship which exists between his own unrestrained sexual gratification and the future welfare of the children. The fertility that Christian tradition exalts is, therefore, rational fertility, not, as is sometimes thought, mere multiplication of offspring in itself.[21]

It is to be feared that on occasion, excessive concentration on the negative side of sex, and on the moral strictures which delimit its use, leads to false or deceptive conclusions. This inadequate approach, which tends to overlook the Church's positive teaching on human reproduction, is not confined to those social scientists who ignore the full range of Christian values; it also extends to some Catholics, who become excessively preoccupied with the moral prohibitions their Church makes known to them.

Something needs to be said at this point about the Church's position on artificial birth control. As indicated at the outset of this paper, the prohibition is not a matter of disciplinary legislation, but a clear pronouncement on the morality of the practice. Such a declaration will not be reversed.

By artificial birth control the Church means the use of any mechanical or chemical contraceptives resorted to for the purpose of keeping the male seed from reaching the uterus and thus penetrating to the Fallopian tubes. The precise type of contraceptive used makes no difference, neither does the established fact that there are differential rates of effectiveness as between the various types.[22] This moral judgement does not change because conception may occasionally occur or even be "planned" despite the habitual use of contraceptives. Rather the moral prohibition extends to each individual use of artificial means designed to frustrate the natural purpose of the act.[23]

Nor is there any contradiction involved in the fact that Catholic moral teaching, while banning the use of contraceptives, in many instances recognizes the legitimacy of marital relations between persons, one or both of whom is incapable of having children. Such would be the case, for instance, with women who have passed the menopause or who are known to be sterile but capable of having intercourse.

The fact that conception will not result from a particular act of intercourse does not render the act unnatural or illicit. In emphasizing this aspect of the natural law, the Church shows conclusively that her first concern is that the reproductive function be not abused by complete exclusion of the primary end of marriage, namely the begetting of children. In her capacity as a moral teacher the Church does not positively advise parents as to the number of children they should have; rather she insists that they regulate their married life in accord with reason and not circumvent the law of nature, as clarified by her, because of the persistence of sexual passion.

Catholicism has judgements in the realm of values and morals regarding contraceptive practices other than the employment of mechanical and chemical means. The governing principle enunciated by moralists is that the act of intercourse must be performed in a natural manner and without the interposition of any positive obstacle to conception. Mechanical and chemical means are ruled out under the second part of that principle, which is, in the last analysis, but a more explicit statement of the first part. In accord with the general principle, Catholic moral thinking also objects to the use of the douche, medicated or unmedicated, as a means of contraception. The relative ineffectiveness of this method does not affect the morality. Even when not used with contraceptive intent, the douche, according to qualified moralists, should not be used immediately following intercourse for a period sufficiently long to give the seed a chance to penetrate the uterus. Behind these seemingly fine distinctions, lies a genuine concern for safeguarding the natural and moral integrity of the reproductive act.

Because it is not in accord with the natural manner of intercourse, coitus interruptus is also ruled out in the Catholic scheme of values affecting human fertility. It is first referred to in Genesis,[24] where the name of Onan provides a name for the practice. Christian tradition, as it is found in the Catholic Church, merely continued the Old Testament ban on onanism. As modern contraceptive techniques developed, the principle underlying the moral objection to onanism was applied and developed.

In line with the same principle, though admittedly not against nature to the same extent, copula dimidiata as a contraceptive technique is rejected by moralists. Its relative ineffectiveness is beside the question.

There are in this connection, many interesting moral discussions on the problems which arise from physical or psychological inability to complete the act of intercourse in the normal manner. The problems involved are not unknown to doctors, psychiatrists and other students of human fertility. Since, however, the question of intended contraception is not prominent in these discussions, there is no reason to give them further attention here.

Contraception is not a new question in Catholic moral discussions, nor do moralists approach it as such. For them today the problem arises from the relative ease with which contraceptive devices and materials can be procured, and information as to their use disseminated. Catholic social thinkers concerned with the family values are realizing progressively that the moral judgements of the average Catholic must be strengthened and his sense of moral values deepened.

It was indicated above that the governing norm whereby various practices in connection with intercourse are evaluated, is the naturalness of the completed act. The likelihood or unlikelihood of contraception on any particular occasion does not in itself affect the morality. There are secondary ends of marriage which justify its legitimate use, even though children do not follow. This reasoning gives rise to questions concerning the moral acceptability of period continence as a means of regulating the number of children. Not a little confusion exists on this subject, and this extends to Catholic circles.[25]

There are two approaches to the use of the "rhythm" of fertility and sterility, or periodic continence, which should be avoided. One is unrestrained advocacy; the other, outright or implied condemnation. As regards the first, it is an inadequate statement of the case to represent periodic continence as just another form of birth control, whereby families can be planned to suit the purely personal wishes of the parents. But it is no less unsatisfactory to discuss the subject in such a way as to leave the impression that rarely if ever, do married couples practice periodic continence without some degree of moral guilt.[26]

As was pointed out above, human fertility is supposed to be reasonable fertility, which in turn implies moral restraint in the use of the reproductive faculties. Some such restraint is obviously associated with the use of periodic continence. Hence, provided unchastity be avoided, taking advantage of the rhythm does not militate against the primary end of marriage in the same way as does artificial birth control or other unnatural practices.

Nevertheless, advocacy of periodic continence must never be such as to obscure or ignore the purpose for which marriage was instituted. Such would be the case were the impression left that rhythm is the Catholic answer to the query of the selfish: How to achieve the gratifications of marriage, while avoiding its major responsibility.

On the other hand, it is unjustifiable to belittle or condemn the use of periodic continence, as some have done, on the grounds that rarely if ever, is the motivation legitimate. The precarious health of a mother, or a well grounded fear that an additional child cannot be cared for properly, are valid reasons for having recourse to such continence. Nor is the motivation of those to be condemned who look ahead and try to foresee how they will care for future offspring. Such an approach to fertility is rational and legitimate, provided of course the parents avoid the opposite error of thinking the fewer the children the better.

Married couples should be informed frankly of the disadvantages which accompany habitual use of the rhythm. In the first place, unless they have attained a high degree of self-restraint, there is likelihood of unchastity by one or other of the parties. Secondly, they should realize that a marriage without children, or with only one or two children, represents an incomplete social institution. Were such marriages common, neither the families nor the social community would replace themselves. Moreover, the resultant psychological strain upon the married couple themselves can create a situation detrimental both to the family and society. It is these undesirable aspects of the arrested family which must be borne in mind when periodic continence is resorted to for purposes of family planning. Even when the motivation is perfectly valid, bad psychological or social effects can result.

The recent social history of our Western civilization indicates that selfishness and baser motives are all too often associated with even a morally legitimate practice like the practice of periodic continence. Instead of a healthy concern that reasonable economic opportunity be afforded children born into this world, we are today witnessing the spread of excessive fear of childbirth and pregnancy, of worry about family living standards to the point where another child is regarded as a tragedy, of too many retarded marriages and unmarried persons in late middle age. In a number of countries of Western civilization, this development is just as much the outcome of selfishness as it is of concern for the welfare of the child.[27]

To what extent to use periodic continence or whether to have recourse to it at all, is a question which cannot be decided by a priori reasoning. Catholicism, as a value system, does not tell parents how many children they must have. Moral attitudes vary, spiritual motivation differs, economic and health considerations are not always the same. Unlike some advocates of planned parenthood, the Catholic Church has learned that ultimate decisions in this matter should be arrived at by the married people themselves. She does not tell them to what extent to use marriage, but declares to them what is morally acceptable and what is not. She counsels them as to the end and nature of marriage, and informs them of their responsibility toward children, and the advisability of moderation. The Church's first concern is that her members do not sin, and then that they should be as reasonable as possible in the ordering of their lives.

There is then, no single simple answer to questions about the rhythm. To try to frame one is to reveal a lack of theological depth, and in addition an ignorance of the findings of the psychological and social sciences. Certainly, it is no answer at all to by-pass the problem, by merely referring to divine Providence. The proper understanding of divine Providence leaves much room for the exercise of human providence, which in turn presupposes the subordination of passion to reason, and in some circumstances the exercise of high and mature virtue.

Admittedly, the delicate adjustment of moral values and motivation in the use of marital continence is not an easy task. There are today all too many Catholic married couples who rationalize their use of the rhythm, and then reveal their moral confusion by attempting to excuse even the employment of artificial birth control techniques. Selfishness, coupled with an excessive desire for sexual gratification, has brought on this confusion. Under these influences the deeper values of Christian self-discipline and

THE CATHOLIC VALUE SYSTEM IN RELATION TO HUMAN FERTILITY

of moderation are obscured.

Yet the spiritual growth of the married couple requires that they learn to integrate into their lives a willingness to accept responsibility and sacrifice, at the same time they acquire reasoned concern for their children's welfare. It should not be forgotten that within the Catholic scheme of values, sacrifice may mean in practice, complete abstinence in some instances from the use of marriage, when no other solution for a problem can be found. Catholicism, over the centuries, has not attempted to win friends for itself by minimizing the difficulties of chaste living. That is a lesson the married need to learn, as well as the unmarried. Their spiritual development requires a proper understanding of the principle involved.

Recommendation of periodic continence should never be such as to upset the delicate balance of moral and spiritual values. It is for this reason that Catholic social thinkers take exception to the commercial exploitation of contemporary knowledge about periodicity without regard for the validity of the motivation. To appeal to fear or selfishness is not only objectionable, it is positively wrong. Similarly, indiscriminate dissemination of information about the details of periodicity, without any concern for proper moral and spiritual guidance, may readily result in spiritual harm to the individuals. Nevertheless, the right of persons entering upon or in the married state, to necessary information, cannot be denied. A qualified person, usually a doctor, can provide the needed technical information; a competent confessor or counselor, the proper moral advice.

At this point it might be noted that perhaps much of the confusion on the subject arises from the difficulty in finding competent guides who integrate in their thinking both the moral principles of governing the use of periodic continence, and an understanding of the spiritual, economic, social and psychological problems which beset married persons in contemporary society. This is but another indication of the urgent need for friendly and intelligent cooperation between the moral and social scientists.

IV. <u>Catholic Values and the Population Problem</u>. It is against this background of doctrinal and moral values that the Catholic social scientist approaches problems of population and resources. His faith emphasizes what reason tells him, namely that the material and spiritual wealth of this world is provided for the benefit of all mankind during the brief span of years within which it is allotted individuals to work out their salvation. The temporal is but a stepping stone to the eternal. Man needs material wealth, but not at the price of losing his soul. Hence, as the Catholic sees it, the morally unacceptable in matters of sex, as well as in other departments of life, cannot be used to solve temporal problems. Ecological difficulties arising from population increase or disequalibrium are no exception.

The question of population in relation to resources is primarily one of quantity not quality, insofar as it relates to human fertility. For that reason, it seems well to omit entirely any discussion of the Catholic position on eugenics, or the studied improvement of quality of population. Insofar as sterilization is concerned, reference has been made above to its illegitimacy for eugenic purposes.[28]

The question of quantity of population in relation to given developed or potential resources, is one which can be treated from either a national or a world viewpoint. From the national viewpoint, few Catholic social thinkers acquainted with the facts would deny that some countries are overpopulated in relation to their present resources, or are in danger of becoming so. Puerto Rico, certain countries of Central America, Italy, and portions of Germany where millions of expellees have resettled, are cases in point.

From a world viewpoint, contemporary Catholic social thought stresses the desirability of a rational reallocation of natural resources in relation to population, and the urgent need for developing new resources and conserving resources already in use. There are, of course, in Catholic circles, as in other portions of the population, persons of an apocalyptic turn of mind who see no solution to the present world situation short of a profound crisis of civilization which would probably result in destruction of millions of human beings and much of our existing resources. These persons may be right, or then again they may not. In any case they are hardly representative of Catholic social thought in general, which stresses the possibilities of social reconstruction and reorganization in such a manner as to allow all peoples access to the natural resources to which they have a right as members of the human community. The world with all its material wealth was made for man, so that the sequestration of its resources by a few individuals or nations, to the detriment of others' rights, is morally indefensible.

It is in accord with Catholic social principles that greater opportunities for movement of peoples should exist. Immigration barriers, when directed less at preservation of social order than at keeping other people from needed resources, are hard to justify.[29] Progressive Catholic

THE CATHOLIC VALUE SYSTEM IN RELATION TO HUMAN FERTILITY

social thought accordingly favors adjustment of immigration laws and of other obstacles, so as to permit a better equilibrium between people and resources to develop in an orderly manner. The unity of Christendom in the Middle Ages, however loosely woven it may have been, is something of an indication how the Christian social philosophy looks beyond the local and national community. In line with its doctrinal beliefs, there is no more ardent defender of a world outlook, or of the brotherhood of man, and of human rights, than the Catholic Church. Hence, it is to be expected that well informed Catholics will appreciate the need for developing a world community in which all men have an opportunity for the satisfaction of temporal needs.

In line with these principles, Catholic social thought regards colonial exploitation of underdeveloped areas, to the detriment of the native populations, as a serious abuse. This is especially true today when the less developed nations stand in great need of learning to use their own resources wisely.[30] Similarly, the Lebensraum theory of Hitler, which saw weaker nations with potential resources, as so many opportunities for raising the living standards of National Socialist Germany, was severely condemned in enlightened Catholic circles. The fact that pro-Mussolini elements attempted to justify on moral grounds the conquest of Ethiopia, is quite apart from authentic social teaching of the Church. Even today the nationalism of some Catholics distorts their understanding of Christian social principles.

But freer movement of peoples cannot be effected, nor natural resources made accessible, without suitable political and economic organization on the international level. This is fully recognized in Catholic social thought, although the Church as such does not make authoritative statements as to the techniques whereby the desired objective can be reached. She merely puts forward the moral principles affecting social organization, and leaves the rest to the political and economic wisdom of men. As a value system, Catholicism will continue to favor reasonable efforts to meet the population and resources problem through international action. Hence, Catholic social thinkers will tend to support development and resettlement projects, reclamation, irrigation and conservation programs, and other morally acceptable plans whereby the world's potential and developed resources can be allocated and distributed to peoples.[31]

There are today, of course, two questions in the minds of all who think about population and resources: (1) Are potential resources adequate to feed the world's people properly for any considerable length of time?

(2) If they are adequate, will men make proper use of the resources to achieve the desired result? As a moral and doctrinal teacher, the Catholic Church does not attempt to give authoritative answers to these questions. What she does say is that men may not resort to unacceptable means to limit population, and that they have a serious obligation in social justice to cooperate in working for increased productivity and a more equitable distribution of material wealth.[32]

In evaluating social behavior, Catholicism takes a midway position between optimism and pessimism. Aware of the fact that original sin has left its effects upon men, and witness over the centuries to the folly, greed and lust of so many human beings, the Catholic Church does not look for a utopia upon earth. But neither, on the other hand, does she take so pessimistic a view of human nature that no hope remains for improvement of conditions through education and cooperative effort.

Brought face to face then, with the temporally important questions about the world's productive capacity and the likelihood of its utilization, the Church assumes the guiding position of a spiritual teacher. She does not formulate programs, but points out directions. Her members do at times support one side or other of the controversy which is currently raging, but their judgements on technical questions must in the last analysis be evaluated on scientific grounds. Meanwhile, the Church carries out her teaching function by insisting upon the doctrinal and moral truths which must be kept in mind when applying economic and social principles to practical programs.

The development of new resources and the proper use of those already developed, according to sound conservation norms, is being stressed increasingly in Catholic social thought. Enlightened resource utilization is now recognized as at least a partial solution to problems created by population pressures. It must be admitted, however, that by and large higher Catholic educational institutions have been slow to grasp the significance of the problems, and to provide courses and research opportunities directed toward more effective conservation and development of resources. Despite the repeated urgings of recent popes, and outstanding efforts of a few pioneers, too many Catholic intellectuals still manifest signs of cultural retardation, when it comes to studying concrete social problems and applying Christian moral principles to their solution. On the elementary school level, however, there are indications in some areas of the United States that as good or better a job is being done as in any other schools. The effects of such training will be felt in the years ahead.[33]

THE CATHOLIC VALUE SYSTEM IN RELATION TO HUMAN FERTILITY

In certain foreign countries with a Catholic cultural tradition, particular difficulties have at times been experienced when efforts were made to arouse the population to better understanding of the need for improved resource utilization. In some of these areas resources have been exploited in a most regrettable manner. This discrepancy between principle and practice should not be laid at the door of the Church as moral teacher. She stresses principles, but does not formulate social policy. In these retarded areas, which have parallels in many non-Christian regions, conflict between Church and State, or undue influence by native Catholic capitalists, often as not, contributed to the situation. On the other hand, it must be recognized that there are other Catholic communities and regions which can be cited as models for enlightened use of land and other natural resources.

Putting aside the question of man's moral obligation to utilize resources intelligently, which today is evident to all whom secularism and laissez-faire have not corrupted, let us turn to a question which is in the minds of many: Is a positive population policy compatible with the Catholic value system? Precisely because the Catholic value system is so many-sided, there is no simple answer. But some inferences can be drawn from what has already been said.

Beginning negatively, it can be stated that the Church will never agree to any morally unacceptable method of population control such as systematic sterilization, legitimized abortion, or dissemination of artificial birth control information and materials. If for prudential reasons, she does not always force these issues, that implies no weakening of disapproval, or any yielding to her disobedient members who may resort to the practices.

On the other hand, Catholicism agrees with those sociologists who exert efforts to eradicate legalized prostitution, easy divorce, child marriage, or hasty entrance into matrimony by immature adolescents. Moreover, so long as pre-marital chastity is properly esteemed, the Catholic value system is not in conflict with the practice of delaying marriage until such time as education has been completed. Actually, in line with all that has been said on the rational use of sex, such delay would in many cases be counselled if there were doubt about the proper support and upbringing of the children. Furthermore, Catholic moral teaching defends the liberty of those who for good reasons do not or cannot marry, insisting merely on their strict obligation to remain chaste and continent, and warning them of the danger of selfishness.

VALUE SYSTEMS AND HUMAN FERTILITY

There is another point worth noting, when it comes to discussion of sex practices in some regions where somewhat different values are set on human fertility, than we are accustomed to in our milieu. Reference is made to areas where very early marriages or high fertility rates are taken for granted regardless of circumstances, or where the custom of irregular marriages or concubinage is prevalent. The full application of Christian teaching on sex would gradually modify the mores of these areas. Within the Catholic scheme of values, chastity holds high place. That means promiscuity and high illegitimacy rates will be affected where these values are accepted. Marriage will be held in greater esteem, and the practice of chaste continence when desirable or necessary, will be more readily approved. The conditions in certain so-called Catholic countries, which are well known to sociologists and students of population, do not reflect the Church's moral teaching. Rather they indicate how the weaknesses of certain cultural patterns persist despite the introduction of religious values. Genuine Christianization of peoples, then, would indirectly work toward a goal many social planners seek, namely stabilization of marriage and a sense of responsibility in making economic provision for offspring.

It can be anticipated that as the Catholic population generally comes to understand better the economic problems attendant upon too rapid population increase, particularly in countries unprepared to support the burden, adjustments in fertility patterns will occur. A sense of social responsibility should operate in a number of cases, just as a sense of individual responsibility toward their own children is evident with most parents. But such a development will be indirect, and the result of people seeing the social scene as it really is in some countries. Catholicism cannot be expected to advocate or approve propaganda calculated to frighten people into planning their families by recourse to periodic continence. In other words, a sense of broadening moral responsibilities may lead married people to practice greater self restraint, but it would be unwise and wrong to put undue pressure upon them or to encourage them to practices which may occasion unchastity because of their weakness. As always, the Church's first concern in these matters is the spiritual welfare of her members. She has no objection to the prudent diffusion of knowledge gained through the social sciences, so that people will acquire a greater sense of social responsibility, but she does not want to see the family undermined or individuals exposed to the danger of unchastity.

In conclusion, let it be said that the Catholic value system will

THE CATHOLIC VALUE SYSTEM IN RELATION TO HUMAN FERTILITY

always place the emphasis upon the primary end of marriage which is the begetting of children. At the same time, it does not deny or overlook the other ends of marriage, among which are to be counted the fostering of mutual love and the quieting of concupiscence. Catholicism does not tell married people they must have a high birthrate, but it does warn them about the abuse of marriage and the dangers of undersized families. It opposes selfishness and excessive individualism, whether it be in the use of sex or in the utilization of material wealth. This is done by insisting upon social responsibility, whether it be to the family or to society in general. Catholicism emphasizes today the need for seeking social solutions for problems of productivity and distribution of material wealth. It sees this procedure as the first approach to difficulties presented by pressure of population upon resources. With family life in the state it is in, Catholicism is frankly concerned that profound values inherent in rational human fertility may be lost sight of, being replaced by a selfish seeking of sex gratification without accompanying regard for the welfare of offspring. Finally, the Catholic value system is not opposed to the systematic study of population problems and of fertility patterns, provided regard be had for ethical values. Rather, the Church welcomes such study, especially when it is accompanied by understanding of the moral truths which underlie the proper use of sex and the reproductive capacity.

The rationale of sex indicated above is not exclusively Catholic. It is founded upon sound natural ethics, and is a reasoned position which the Catholic Church has merely defended and, where necessary, clarified.

VALUE SYSTEMS AND HUMAN FERTILITY

FOOTNOTES

1. As regards the relationship between the moral and the social sciences, Pius XI might here be cited: "Certainly the Church was not given the commission to guide men to an only fleeting and perishable happiness but to what is eternal. Indeed 'the Church holds that it is unlawful for her to mix without cause in these temporal concerns' (Pius XI, encyclical Ubi Arcano, Dec. 23, 1922); however, she can in no wise renounce the duty God entrusted to her to interpose her authority, not of course in matters of technique for which she is neither suitably equipped nor endowed by office, but in all things that are connected with the moral law. . .Even though economics and moral science employs each its own principles in its own sphere, it is, nevertheless, an error to say that the economic and moral orders are so distinct from and alien to each other that the former depends in no way on the latter. Certainly the laws of economics, as they are termed, being based on the very nature of material things and on the capacities of the human body and mind, determine the limits of what productive human effort cannot, and of what it can attain in the economic field and by what means. Yet it is reason itself that clearly shows, on the basis of the individual and social nature of things and of men, the purpose which God ordained for all economic life." Pius XI, Encyclical Quadragesimo Anno (on reconstructing the social order), May 15, 1931. Translation is that of the National Catholic Welfare Conference edition (1942), p.17.

2. "Not only is it impossible for faith and reason to be at odds, but rather they mutually aid each other, since right reason makes clear the foundations of faith and in its light develops an orderly knowledge of things divine, and faith frees reason and safeguards it from errors, while providing it with a multiple source of knowledge." Vatican Council, Session III, Ch. 4. Latin text in Denzinger-Umberg-Bannwart, Enchiridion Symbolorum. Fribourg, Herder. No. 1799.

3. The Vatican Council made it clear that the Roman Pontiff when he speaks ex cathedra, that is authoritatively in virtue of his office as supreme pastor and teacher, enjoys the same infallibility with which Christ wished His Church to be endowed when it defined doctrines of faith or morals. Cf. the Latin text in Denzinger-Umberg-Bannwart, op. cit. No. 1839.

4. Pius XII made this point in a series of three annual addresses on the nature of ecclesiastical authority to the Sacred Roman Rota at its opening sessions in 1945, 1946 and 1947. See especially the address of 1947. Cf. Acta Apostolicae Sedis 39: 493-498; and English translation in The Clergy Review 29: 196-200.

5. The French ethician, Jacques Leclercq, has put the matter thus: "Moral obligation corresponds to the notion of an order established by creative intelligence and imposing itself upon human reason. The good, for each and everything, is to be in its own place within the order. Moral good is the subordination of man's free activity to the order willed by God." In a footnote he adds: "Some will probably be surprised that we omit the idea of permission and prohibition, since so many regard a good act as one that is permitted, and a bad act as one that is forbidden. But in order to reduce this conception of moral good and evil to the one given above, all that it is necessary to do is to analyze the notion of permission and prohibition. God, nature's Author, has created man with the nature he possesses for the purpose of having him attain happiness through the perfection of his nature. Man, by developing himself in conformity with his nature, tends at

one and the same time toward perfection and happiness. Accordingly, prescribed acts are those which are necessary because they are required for man's development; permitted acts are those which are conformable to man's development but are not strictly demanded of it; and forbidden acts are those which are opposed to man's development. As St. Thomas put it, 'We do not wrong God unless we wrong our own good.' Summa Contra Gentiles, Bk. III, Ch. 122." Jacques Leclercq, Marriage and the Family; a study in social philosophy. New York, Pustet, 1945. P. 117.

6. How difficult is the subjecting of passion to reason, the Catholic tradition fully recognizes. "It is hard to be a rational animal and to direct one's body by one's soul even to the depths of one's being, even to the point where the will engages itself in the organism. A man must labor and bleed in order to purify and spiritualize slowly those shadowy regions where the past of our species and of ourselves has allowed too many evil roots to sink in." Emil Mersch. Morality and the Mystical Body. P.J. Kennedy, 1939. P. 224. The excerpt is from the author's penetrating essay,"Love, Marriage and Chastity."

7. Cf. 1 Corinthians 7: 25-35, where St. Paul outlines the Christian evaluation of virginity.

After urging upon a group of women the duty of preparing themselves properly for the duties of the married state, the present pope, Pius XII, continued as follows: "But let us remember that for nigh on to twenty centuries, thousands and thousands of men and women, from among the best, in order to follow the counsels of Christ, freely renounced the possibility of a family of their own and the sacred duties and rights of married life." Pius XII, Address on Woman's Duties in Social and Political Life. Paulist press edition (1945), p. 6.

8. Arthur Vermeersch, S.J. De Castitate. 2d ed. Rome, Gregorian University, 1926. P. 57.

9. Speaking of this aspect of married life, Pius XI said: "God wishes men to be born not only that they should live and fill the earth, but much more that they may be worshippers of God, that they may know Him and love Him and finally enjoy Him forever in heaven; and this end, by reason of man's being raised by God in a marvelous way to the supernatural order, surpasses all that eye hath seen, and ear heard, and all that hath entered into the heart of man." Pius XI, Encyclical, Casti Connubii (on Christian marriage) December 31, 1930. Translation is from America press edition (1936), p. 5.

10. The common teaching of the Church on the possibility of fulfilling the moral law, even under hardship, has been summarized by the Council of Trent: "Let none be so rash as to assert that which the Fathers of the Council have placed under anathema, namely, that there are precepts of God impossible for the just to observe. God does not ask the impossible, but by His commands, instructs you to do what you are able, to pray for what you are not able, that He may help you." Session VI, Chapter XI. Latin text in Denzinger-Umberg-Bannwart, op. cit. No. 804.

11. Jacques Leclercq. op. cit. P. 98. In a footnote reference is made to St Thomas, Summa Theologica, II, II, q. 151, a.1.

12. For a fuller discussion of the relationship of self-restraint to chastity and marriage, see Leclercq, op. cit. P. 137 ff.

13. "The primary end of marriage is the procreation and education of children; the secondary end, mutual comfort and the remedy of concupiscence." Code of Canon Law, canon 1013, No. 1.

14. Jacques Leclercq, op. cit. P. 104-105.

15. "Let it be repeated as an unchanged and inviolable fundamental doctrine that matrimony was not instituted or restored by man but by God; not by man were the laws made to strengthen and confirm and elevate it but by God, the Author of nature, and by Christ our Lord by whom nature was redeemed, and hence these laws cannot be subject to any human decrees or to any contrary pact even of the spouses themselves." Pius XI, Encyclical *Casti Connubii*, December 31, 1930. Translation from America press edition (1936), p. 2.

16. "Public magistrates have no direct power over the bodies of their subjects. Therefore, where no crime has taken place and there is no cause present for grave punishment, they can never directly harm, or tamper with the integrity of the body, either for the reason of eugenics or for any other reason. St. Thomas teaches this when, inquiring whether human judges for the sake of preventing future evils can inflict punishment, he admits that the power indeed exists as regards certain forms of punishment, but justly and properly denies it as regards the maiming of the body: 'No one who is guiltless may be punished by a human tribunal either by flogging to death, mutilation, or by beating.'

"Furthermore, Christian doctrine establishes, and the light of human reason makes it most clear, that private individuals have no other power over the members of their bodies than that which pertains to their natural ends; and they are not free to destroy or mutilate their members, or in any way render themselves unfit for their natural functions, except when no other provision can be made for the good of the whole body." Pius XI, Encyclical *Casti Connubii*, December 31, 1930. Translation from America press edition (1936), p. 21-22.

17. Guy Irving Burch and Elmer Pendell. *Human Breeding and Survival* (Population Roads to Peace and War). Penguin Books, 1947. P. 87 ff.

18. Latin text in *Acta Apostolicae Sedis*, 32: 73; Holy Office, 24 Feb., 1940. Cf. also T.L. Bouscaren, *Canon Law Digest*, Vol. II, canon 247.

19. Jacques Leclercq, op. cit. P. 210.

20. St. Thomas, commenting on Augustine says categorically: "Continence would not have been laudable in the state of innocence, whereas it is praiseworthy at the present time—not indeed on account of the consequent absence of fecundity, but on account of its removal of inordinate lust. But in that other state there would have been fecundity without lust." *Summa Theologica*, I, q. 98, a. 2, ad 3.

For a full discussion of the matter, see Vol. 2, chapters 2 and 3, of E.C. Messenger's *Two in One Flesh*, Westminister, Md., Newman press, 1948. 3 vols.

21. Jacques Leclerq, op. cit. P. 214, and also p. 211, footnote.

22. In this connection there is the study by Regine K. Stix, M.D., "A Comparative Appraisal of Three Contraceptive Services," in *The Journal of the American Medical Association*, 118: 283-290, January 24, 1942. There were published two earlier studies along the same line: "Effectiveness of Birth Control," by Regine K. Stix, M.D., and Frank W. Notestein, *Milbank Memorial Fund Quarterly*, 12: 57-68, January, 1934; and "Effectiveness of Birth Control: A Second Study of Contraceptive Practice in a Selected Group of New York Women," by Regine K. Stix, M.D. and Frank W. Notestein, *Milbank Memorial Fund Quarterly*, 13:162-178, April, 1935.

23. "But no reason, however grave, may be put forward by which anything intrinsically against nature may become conformable to nature and morally good. Since, therefore, the conjugal act is destined primarily by nature for

the begetting of children, those who in exercising it deliberately frustrate its natural power and purpose, sin against nature and commit a deed which is shameful and intrinsically vicious . . . Any use whatsoever of matrimony exercised in such a way that the act is deliberately frustrated in its natural power to generate life is an offense against the law of God and of nature, and those who indulge in such are branded with the guilt of grave sin." Pius XI, Encyclical *Casti Connubii*, December 31, 1930. Translation from America press edition (1936), p. 17.

24. Genesis 38: 8-10.

25. See, for example, the June, 1948 issue of *Integrity* (Vol. 2, no. 9) which was devoted to the subject, "Children, More or Less."

26. "Nor are those considered as acting against nature who in the married state use their rights in the proper manner although on account of natural reasons either of time or of certain defects, new life cannot be brought forth. For in matrimony as well as in the use of the matrimonial rights there are secondary ends, such as mutual aid, the cultivation of mutual love, and the quieting of concupiscence, which husband and wife are not forbidden to intend so long as the intrinsic nature of the act is preserved." Pius XI, Encyclical *Casti Connubii*. America press edition, p. 18.

27. Jacques Leclercq, op. cit. P. 152.

28. See quotation from Encyclical *Casti Connubii*, in footnote 16 above.

29. In this connection the entire Pentecost (1941) address of Pius XII should be read. Composed in the midst of war, it emphasizes what international statesmen clearly recognize, that ecological disequilibrium of a serious nature is a standing invitation to armed conflict between nations.

30. The 1948 Semaine Sociale de France was devoted to the topic: *Les Peuples d'Outre-Mer*. These annual social weeks take up contemporary problems of national and international import, and endeavor to apply Christian principles to their solution.

31. An example of one kind of adjustment envisioned by at least some Catholic writers is the following: "Reasonable provision must be made for outlets in the case of countries of rapidly increasing population. When additional space for necessary emigration is honestly needed, when the pressure is authentic and natural, not alleged or artificial, negotiations should ensue before some competent tribunal with compensation and protection guaranteed to the conceding power. Otherwise brute force and the hysteria of peoples propagandized into a conviction of injury will plunge the world into reciprocal slaughter and atomic chaos. A more equitable access to and control of essential raw materials in the world must, moreover, replace the virtual monopoly previously exercised by the favored few. Narrow exploitation of the rarer but necessary ingredients of modern industrial production which are found by accident of nature within the jurisdiction of America, England, Japan, Russia, China, Canada or Bolivia can no longer be reconciled with the economic liberalism now assumed as the cornerstone of international peace. It will be futile to control atomic energy without first disciplining and spiritualizing the will and the intellect and the conscience of explosive human atoms." Edmund A. Walsh, S.J. *Total Power*. Doubleday, 1948. P. 48.

32. Pius XI, in the Encyclical *Quadragesimo Anno*, May 15, 1931, laid great stress upon the social character of property, as a corrective to the excessive individualism which too long influenced much Christian social thought. ". . . however the earth may be apportioned among private owners, it does not cease to serve the common good of all. This same

doctrine We ourselves also taught just above in declaring that the division of goods which results from private ownership was established by nature itself in order that created things may serve the needs of mankind in a fixed and stable order. Lest one wander from the right path of truth, this is something which must be continually kept in mind. But not every distribution among human beings of property and wealth is of a character to attain either completely or with a satisfactory degree of perfection, the ends which God intended. Therefore the riches which socio-economic development constantly increase ought to be so distributed among individual persons and classes that the common advantage of all, which Leo XIII had praised, will be safeguarded; in other words, that the common good of all society will be kept inviolate. By this law of social justice, one man is forbidden to exclude the other from sharing in the benefits." Pius XI, Encyclical Quadragesimo Anno, paragraphs 56 and 57, quoted in William Feree, Introduction to Social Justice. Paulist press, 1948. P. 13.

33. Efforts of the National Catholic Rural Life Conference have been at least partially responsible for the development. This group, founded twenty-five years ago by Bishop Edwin V. O'Hara of Kansas City, Mo., then a priest, has for a long time urged proper resource utilization as a duty of stewardship and social justice. Studying the problem of Catholics' flight from the land as well as the differential birthrate, it naturally became interested in the question of population and resources. Monsignor Luigi G. Ligutti, its executive secretary, is also official observer for the Holy See to the Food and Agricultural Organization of the United Nations. This new relationship with a technical international body concerned with agricultural resources and food production, indicates the growing interest in the problem at the Vatican.

VALUES, POPULATION, AND THE SUPERNATURAL: A CRITIQUE[1]

Kingsley Davis
Columbia University

Habituated to the statistical handling of tangible facts, modern demographers show little facility in dealing with the ethical realm. They usually ignore ethical values, and if they do touch upon them, they tend to become evaluative themselves or to ascribe to values a significance beyond the capacity of science to understand or measure. Yet values, by almost any definition, are deeply involved in the behavior governing births and deaths in human society, and like other phenomena they are susceptible to scientific analysis. Although the student of social structure is more at home in dealing with ethical values than is the demographer, he is too often unfamiliar with demographic facts and techniques. Accordingly, it is refreshing to have a populationist like Dr. Taeuber who has an unusual knowledge of comparative sociology, and a historian like Professor Russell who knows a great deal about population, address themselves directly to the demographic significance of human values.

The common belief that values cannot be scientifically studied rests seemingly on their subjectivity and their controversiality. It is hard to get agreement even on a working definition of the term "value." None of the three papers under consideration faces this difficulty squarely. In consequence the discussion is somewhat confused. The first paper justifiably asks whose values are mainly significant in influencing the reproductive behavior of the Asiatic masses, and seems to answer the question by devoting primary attention to the peasant mores. The second paper takes the "supreme worth of the human soul" and the "superior value of human dignity" as the keys to medieval values, but subsequently relies upon social and economic organization to explain the actual demographic situation. Thus the emphasis is shifted in both cases from values as such to the institutions and norms which presumably embody the relevant values. Such a shift is understandable because, especially with reference to historical materials, the actual social organization affords one of the best indices of subjective motivation. Yet it is worth noting that, in the common meaning of the term, a value can exist quite apart from its embodiment in practice. An alcoholic may believe firmly in the value of abstention. At the risk of seeming elementary, therefore, one should be clear that an ethical or valuational proposition is a statement of preference, not a statement of fact. If this much is agreed upon, a clear distinction can be made between the last of our three papers and the first two. The first two are attempts to speak about value systems from the standpoint of an outside observer anxious to understand their bearing on demographic behavior. The third paper, on the contrary, is an attempt to speak about a value system from the standpoint of an insider who presumably shares the values discussed; its purpose is to persuade the reader that the values are "right," utilizing for this end both statements of alleged fact (some supernatural and some natural) and statements of sentiment and attitude. Between the two approaches—that of the observer and that of the believer—there is no reconciliation. To be sure, the scientific observer cannot quarrel with the preferences of the believer; if he does, if he tells the believer what values he _should_ have, he ceases to be a scientific observer. However, the observer can, and indeed as a scientist he must, quarrel with any supposedly existential statements he believes to be untrue; and since every value system tends to bolster itself with an alleged description of what the world is actually like, the scientific and the religio-ethical approaches are perpetually at war, despite any facile proclamations to the contrary. For the purpose of the present critique, therefore, the third paper must be viewed as an _example_, not an analysis, of a system of values. It cannot be criticized by an outside observer in terms of the preferences or values it expresses, but solely in terms of the facts it alleges and the logic it employs. The claim, for example, that the church is divinely appointed to exercise authority over the morality of mankind is obviously not susceptible of scientific proof. Anyone who accepts it does so on faith—faith in the supernatural. If one views with scientific scepticism the supernatural propositions of Father Gibbons' paper, the deductions from these propositions also fall down. The only thing left then for our serious consideration is what effect the views of the church may have upon actual demographic behavior.

In Dr. Taeuber's paper two points require particular mention. The first is that, at least for the East, we know very little about the beliefs and values of the illiterate peasant masses. The reason: almost no scientific research has been done on the subject. Yet modern techniques of attitude and opinion measurement could certainly be applied to get the facts, and

VALUES, POPULATION, AND THE SUPERNATURAL: A CRITIQUE

the cost (not too great if sampling is used) should be justified in view of the importance of population problems in the Orient. In the absence of research, as Dr. Taeuber points out, there has been too much reliance upon the "philosophical and ethical pronouncements of the great leaders" as evidence of the values involved in demographic behavior. Professor Russell bears out the same point by telling us that there were *two* sets of values in the Middle Ages, one held by the clergy, the other by the laity— the first set being much better documented than the second.

These observations lead us to the second point—namely, that the ethical and religious formulations of specialized groups may have only a negligible influence on the demographic behavior of the masses. The formulations of a self-contained class of professional theologians or philosophers are generally couched in abstract terms, are usually a few centuries behind the times, take little account of the actual conditions faced by the ordinary person, and in practice are capable of varied interpretations to suit the convenience of the situation. One could not predict from the sacred literature of the Hindus the demographic behavior of the Indian people, any more than one could predict from Catholic doctrine the actual behavior of either medieval or contemporary Catholics. This means not only that other things besides values influence behavior, but also that other values than those mummified in official doctrine are at work.

Reflection on history leaves the impression that the reproductive folkways and mores of the common man have varied more in relation to the conditions of his life than with reference to religious or philosophical doctrine. Although contraception has become a Western folkway, no major religion advocated its use *prior* to its popular adoption. The common people took it over in the face of almost universal ecclesiastical opposition. Today the official Catholic doctrine on this matter is not preventing the widespread use of contraception by Catholics. It seems that, when other factors are similar, Catholics in the United States use contraception slightly less than do Protestants and Jews; but as compared to factors such as degree of urbanization, education, income, etc., the influence of Catholic affiliation is not strong. In Latin America the Catholic views on concubinage and illegitimacy do not prevent these institutions from being widespread. In view of this discrepancy between official religio-ethical values and the actual ones pursued by the people, it seems likely that the hair-splitting distinction between "natural" and "artificial" methods of limiting offspring will have little influence on the behavior of the Catholic masses throughout the world. How long the Catholic clergy will lay down one rule while its parishioners follow another is hard to say. The church is now obviously in a difficult position, and it is quite possible that if new techniques of contraception are invented, it may adapt itself to the modern world by giving the new techniques its sanction, finding some acceptable theological reason for doing so and yet forbidding the ones it has already banned.

To people concerned over the misery of densely settled and rapidly increasing agricultural populations, any pronouncement from any major religion is of considerable importance. Even though formal religious doctrine may not exercise a major influence, such people are still looking for help from any quarter which will aid in reducing the fertility of overpopulated regions. Father Gibbons' paper will therefore be read with interest. What does it offer? It emphasizes that the church does not advocate unrestricted reproduction within marriage. This is favorable for the people in question. But it also says that postponement of marriage, the "rhythm" method, and in general "self-control" are the only methods allowable. In view of this extreme limitation on the means, our people concerned with overpopulation may question the sincerity of the church's interest in the population problem, especially since the church makes every effort, through legislative lobbying, to force its restrictions on the general public. The view that people who use mechanical and chemical contraceptives are less self-controlled than those who do not will find scant support from those who are worried about densely settled impoverished regions. It will seem to them that the individuals who have the greatest civic and social responsibility are precisely those who practice efficient contraception, that the aim of such individuals is not to have no children at all, not to have limitless intercourse, but simply to have a socially satisfactory size of family.

Further, many will question whether the substantial body of opinion cited by Father Gibbons as favoring redistribution of the world's resources and freer movement of the earth's people offers any solution to the world's long-range population problem. An equalization of the world's resources as between regions would merely postpone the time of reckoning when either population would have to stop growing or the standard of living would have to decline. Equality does not itself create wealth. It seems beyond question that the earth's human population cannot go on increasing forever. Simple arithmetic will show that in just a few centuries the current rate of increase would cover the earth's crust solidly with human flesh, and eventually the entire substance of the earth would be absorbed into the bodies of human beings. The growth must stop at some point, and there are only two things that can stop it: a decline in fertility or a rise in mortality. If the church

VALUES, POPULATION, AND THE SUPERNATURAL: A CRITIQUE

persists in forbidding the more efficient means of reducing fertility, it will be open to the accusation that it is really favoring high mortality. The church's position is still reminiscent of the time when death rates were so high that, as Dr. Taeuber states, the need was to achieve a fertility high enough to ensure survival. The need today, in many regions at least, is to achieve a fertility low enough to ensure a decent standard of living. For this need the church has an ideal solution— celibacy and continence— but one that is objectionable to many millions on moral and psychiatric grounds and which has never yet been proved workable. As a consequence, another solution has been adopted by the peoples of the West and is being looked for in connection with the peoples of the East.

FOOTNOTE

1. This is, in somewhat expanded form, the prepared discussion presented at the session on "Value Systems and Human Fertility."

SECTION V

FUTURE COURSE OF RESEARCH IN FERTILITY

Afternoon Session, May 29, 1949
Clyde V. Kiser, Milbank Memorial Fund, Chairman

PHYSIOLOGICAL FACTORS AND THEIR CONTROL

Howard C. Taylor, Jr., M.D.
Columbia University

As a teacher of Obstetrics and Gynecology it seems to me not inappropriate that I should be addressing your association. The work of my branch of medicine certainly should furnish you with data on physiologic mechanisms and on individual clinical behavior which must be necessary for your complete understanding of your subject matter. We, on the other hand, need your experience in order to see the social results of our work and, in some degree, to understand its objectives.

I am sure that as a single speaker, representing an experience outside of the usual range of population study, that you want from me only a quick, and necessarily superficial, survey of present medical thinking and a report of some of the more significant recent advances in the physiologic aspects of the control of fertility.

Ovulation: It is natural to start with the ovum and the process of ovulation when the egg cell is extruded from the ovary and starts its six inch, six day journey through the Fallopian tube to the point at which it becomes embedded in the uterine lining. Many new facts have been learned about this process in recent years and some groping efforts made toward its regulation.

The final impulse which produces ovulation has been known for some years to be a chemical one based on a substance or substances manufactured by the anterior pituitary gland. These substances have been isolated and partly purified, and in laboratory animals in a receptive physiologic state, ovulation can be artificially produced at the will of the investigator. In the human subject the relationships are more complex and the available anterior pituitary gonadotropic substances have been a disappointment in that they have failed to produce ovulation in sterile women.

Ovulation may also be prevented by employing other chemical substances, both in laboratory animals and in man. The specific products of the sex glands themselves belong to a group of compounds called steroids.

FUTURE COURSE OF RESEARCH IN FERTILITY

Whether estrogens from the ovary or androgens from the testis they have the ability to check the activity of the anterior pituitary gland in either sex and so prevent ovulation. It is thus quite possible by administering large doses of one of these hormones in the first part of the menstrual cycle to render a woman temporarily sterile. As a contraceptive measure the method has not been given practical application. The substances are expensive. The effect, although temporary, is not known to be without permanent results if used over a long period of time. Finally the action of these steroids is not limited to the control of the anterior pituitary's ovulation producing function, but may have far reaching general physiologic effects, such for example an influence on the periodicity of the menstrual cycle. Could a chemical variant of one of these hormones be found with a physiologic effect devoted only to the inhibition of ovulation that much sought after agent, the "ideal contraceptive" would be found. This is a remote possibility, however, because the various physiologic phases of the reproductive cycle are so interrelated that it seems unlikely that one, notably ovulation, could be suppressed without upsetting the entire mechanism.

A perhaps more practical discovery has been the observation that the process of ovulation is accompanied by a minute but nevertheless detectible rise in the body temperature. It has of course long been known that ovulation occurs in the middle of the menstrual interval, the mode being on the fourteenth day. Individual as well as monthly variations may put ovulation as early as the 8th or as late as the 20th day of the cycle. Now it also appears probable that the life of both sperm and free ovum is short, probably 12 to 48 hours for each. Fertilization is therefore possible during only two or three days each month. The problem has been to determine which two days, these to be avoided for those fearing pregnancy and to be sought by those desiring it.

The keeping of daily so called basal body temperature records is part of every therapeutic regime for the treatment of sterility, a somewhat onerous undertaking which at least provides a test of the patient's conviction that she wants children. As a means of making more accurate the "safe period" as a technique of contraception it has not proved of great value. The curves of the temperature variation may show that ovulation has occurred and that the remainder of the month is relatively "safe." It cannot predict an impending ovulation, however, and the first part of the cycle is therefore still somewhat insecure. Nevertheless the fact remains that according to present physiologic beliefs, conception is scarcely possible

PHYSIOLOGICAL FACTORS AND THEIR CONTROL

before the eighth or after the twentieth day of a 28 day cycle. When failures occur it probably means that arithmetic or memory, rather than biology, is at fault and very many women are certainly basing a successful birth control program on the safe period method.

<u>The Testis</u>: At this point it may be well to refer briefly to advances in the knowledge of the male aspects of the fertility problem. Contrary to earlier beliefs male sterility is fairly common and certainly accounts for at least a third of sterile human matings. The causes of male sterility are in part obstructions in ducts, due as a rule to past infections, and more commonly to defects in the sperm cells themselves.

The techniques for examining the sperm have developed rapidly in recent years so that now a half dozen characteristics, including the number of sperm per cubic centimeter of seminal fluid, the motility and the presence of abnormal forms are recorded in a routine test.

Various agents and conditions are known to affect deleteriously the quantity and quality of the sperm. These include psychologic factors of worry and fatigue, gamma radiation from any source, nutritive deficiencies concerned particularly with certain amino acids and again the steroid sex hormones of either ovary or testis when given in very large amounts. The possibility may be envisaged here, as for the ovary, of an "ideal" chemical contraceptive, the problem being to find an agent whose action is limited to this single function and whose effect is temporary.

Implantation of Ovum and Early Abortion

To return to the recently fertilized ovum, one finds an extraordinary increase in our knowledge of the first two weeks of human history. This was stimulated by work on monkeys carried out at the Carnegie Institute in Baltimore where fertilized ova were found and examined on successive days after known dates of mating. The later human studies were made by Drs. Rock and Hertig of Harvard Medical College who for a decade have been making a systematic search of gynecologic surgical specimens of uteri for ova and have collected a considerable series of very young fertilized human eggs in the process of migration through the genital tract and the beginning of their implantation in the uterine wall. Their work has established an average of six days time required for the ovum to reach its resting place on the uterine wall. It has also shown that a considerable portion of all fertilized eggs are defective and many biologic abortions occur before a delay in the menstrual period has signaled the possibility of a pregnancy.

The cause of these very early abortions as well as the later more apparent ones has important implications. At least a tenth and perhaps a fifth of all pregnancies terminate in this way, accounting for a fetal loss of perhaps 400,000 annually in the United States. This is a major medical problem. From another viewpoint factors affecting the ovum that would result in its destruction before the first menstrual period might be admissible as contraceptive measures, although even from a biologic standpoint this is at present a purely theoretical possibility.

Until recently it was held that abortions resulted from congenital defects in the primitive cells of the ovary or testis. This view was supported by studies of aborted embryos which showed that the majority were anatomically defective. These observations produced a somewhat fatalistic attitude toward abortions, which were regarded as predestined at the time of the union of an inadequate sperm or ovum. Abortions under this theory could therefore not be prevented by medical means.

These views have been somewhat changed by the observation that certain agents, particularly radiation, the virus of German measles and probably other viruses, acting on the embryo during the first three months of pregnancy will result in babies born alive at term but with characteristic congenital defects. From this observation it is but a step to the acceptance of the possibility that similar agents acting still earlier in the course of pregnancy might result in fetal injury from which abortion must occur. The theory that abortion frequently arises from unfavorable uterine environment, rather than from preconceptional germ plasm defects is thus revived. Whether attempts should be made to control fertility by affecting the uterine environment and thus producing extremely early abortions is perhaps more a sociologic than a biologic or medical question.

Contraceptive Agents

A word must be said in passing about the status of common birth control practices. Mechanical methods have, except for some improvement in materials, changed little in the last decade. The vaginal diaphragm is widely accepted by physicians and birth control clinics in the New York area. Whether this indicates absolute superiority to other mechanical devices or is largely a matter of fashion cannot, I think, be definitely stated.

Chemical agents have apparently improved somewhat on the basis of biological and biophysical study of sperm behavior. This has been largely, but not entirely, the accomplishment of the laboratories of certain pharmaceutical houses. Further progress, if it comes, may on account of relatively large funds available be expected from such sources.

PHYSIOLOGICAL FACTORS AND THEIR CONTROL

Whether the reliability of contraceptive measures as applied and practiced has increased in the last twenty years is uncertain. Probably it has to a degree. The record of our own hospital sterility clinic is that a normal expectancy of 80 pregnancies per 100 woman years of exposure can be reduced to about 12 or possibly 6 if certain corrections are allowed. This clinic depends on a lower middle class urban population of only moderate education; but all of us who practice medicine know that there are many contraceptive failures even in the highest economic groups and in those with the best education.

Surgical Measures for Sterilization

In the consideration of fertility control it is important, finally, not to overlook the effects that the perfection of surgical methods may have on this whole problem. Within the last decade the improvement of anesthetics, the development of transfusion techniques and the discovery of penicillin have made possible formerly inconceivable operations and have reduced the mortality from all major procedures. Less dramatically, they have nearly eliminated the risk and discomforts of less formidable, standard surgical operations.

This has had far reaching effects. Among others has been the rise in the permissible figure for cesarean section, now at 6 per cent in our hospital and at a higher figure in other institutions. It has also made acceptable a procedure, which fifteen years ago, would certainly have been frowned upon, namely postpartum sterilization. This is an operation readily performed either in the delivery room itself or within the first few days of the puerperium. At this time the enlarged uterus brings the tubes close to the abdominal wall which is itself thinned by the preceding pregnancy. An incision only an inch or two in length affords access to the tubes which can be ligated without significant risk or discomfort and the patient can be discharged from the hospital on the usual postpartum day. The method is certain, and is effective regardless of economic or educational status of the patient. It is a method which can be applied wherever it is customary for women to be hospitalized for delivery and where prejudices are not too rigid for people to consent to the procedure after a family of reasonable size has been obtained. It is possible that our attention should be directed as much to the hospital as to the chemical laboratory for the solution of the contraception problem.

Let me in closing repeat my conviction of the need that the medical profession should have some of your knowledge and should to some extent participate in the attempt to solve your problems.

AN APPROACH TO RESEARCH
IN OVERCOMING CULTURAL BARRIERS TO FAMILY LIMITATION

Clarence Senior
Columbia University

That value systems influence human behavior, including its fertility aspects, has been well pointed out in the preceding papers. That an understanding of the values supplied by any society for its members must be a major concern of demographers is a truism. There is no dispute on the necessity for research in this field, and in recent years there have been many noteworthy studies upon which social scientists can draw in understanding differential fertility both at home and abroad. Of late, great stress has been placed upon the pre-industrial areas of the globe, and it is with them that I am mainly concerned.

The institutions and the values of pre-industrial societies have long stressed large families as a necessary condition for perpetuation of the group. We know that peoples living in the pre-Pasteur era must assure their survival in just such a wasteful "natural" manner. We know the general outlines of the values and institutions of most of the world include rural feudalism, class and caste rigidities, traditional values attached to time, income, and leisure, localism arising from relative isolation, a subordinate position for women, and a church which supports the undemocratic structure. It may do so consciously, as in much of Latin America where it has intervened openly on the side of the ruling class for centuries, or it may do so by preaching the doctrine which Father Gibbons stated so succinctly, that the mission of man was "the achievement of beatitude in the life to come."

A classic statement of the demographer's attitude toward the problems of lowering fertility in these areas of rapid population increase is that of Notestein:

> "The dissemination of contraceptive knowledge as the sole solution to the problems of population pressure is of little importance. . . . Contraception is an important means, among others, by which people can control their fertility. Whether they control it depends on the

social setting; hence new patterns of behavior are to be established principally by the alteration of that setting." [1]

We must agree with the statement, but it, as well as many similar ones, is too often understood as implying that it will take several centuries for the whole complex of Western European capitalist industrialism to be transferred to the "backward" areas and that only then will fertility be brought under control. If we have to wait to "let nature take its course" we can confidently look forward to the catastrophes foreseen by Vogt, Osborne, et al.

1. A vast field of demographic research is opened up if we follow through the question, "Do culture complexes travel as wholes, or can specific traits be spread faster than the complex as a whole?" The recent work of sociologists studying the spread of industry will give us important leads.[2] Professor Notestein himself, in the paper quoted, has outlined an important program with which to attack the problems of population pressure. The factors in the differential diffusion of Western culture need careful analysis. It has often been pointed out that we have introduced the techniques of death control but have withheld the techniques of birth control. The influence of the church in the imperial countries is undoubtedly important in this respect, but it certainly is not the only factor involved. What can be done today in the twilight of imperialism and the dawn of world organization which could not be done yesterday? What can be done by democracies which could not be done by the unenlightened and unrepresentative metropolitan governments of the past? These questions need deep exploration.

2. Another general field needing examination is the study of how individuals actually behave while still holding themselves to be acting within the limits of the received value system and its institutional expressions. Certainly, after the Kinsey report, no one can remain unaware of the tremendous range of difference between classes, regions, educational levels, etc. in the interpretation of the Judeo-Christian moral precepts and values by which we in the United States presumably are bound. While the range is undoubtedly less among pre-industrial peoples, there is every reason to believe that variation from the norms is found in every society but the most isolated and "static." Such variation, testified to by many anthropologists, should be adopted as a generalized research lead into the possibilities of increasing the variation. Let me illustrate what is possible by a hasty account of certain factors in the spread of the practice of sterilization in Puerto Rico, an island famous for its high fertility, on which the Catholic

FUTURE COURSE OF RESEARCH IN FERTILITY

Church claims a membership of at least 85 per cent of the population.

Some 25 or 30 years ago, sterilization began to be practiced by upper class women as a birth control measure. The operation, at that time, was both hazardous and costly. It filled a need, however. The women wanted to go to confession but not have to confess the use of mechanical methods of preventing conception. The rationalization which one finds generally made is that sterilization, being one "sin," is forgiven at the next occasion for penance, whereas the use of contraceptives would entail a constant series of confessions and penances! Many of the same women who thus solved their own problem were bitterly opposed to the introduction of public clinics where the wives of workers and peasants could solve theirs. However, in spite of church opposition, the insular legislature legalized contraception for health purposes, including sterilization, in 1937.

It happens that the physical difficulties of birth control on the island are great. They are at least as serious an obstacle to controlled fertility as are the cultural barriers.[3] Sterilization is looked upon by many as a short-cut which will obviate such difficulties as lack of running water, absence of privacy, shortage of nurses and doctors, etc. Recent advances have reduced the cost and the danger, especially as a post-partum operation.

Gradually, the practice began to spread down from the upper class women to the urban working class families, but of course the problem is far more serious in the country than in the cities. The idea was spread in the rural areas in a most illuminating manner. After a clinic up in the mountains had performed a dozen or so sterilizations, it was attacked in a pastoral letter. The reading of the letter in the rural churches was followed by a wave of inquiries at public health clinics and to private doctors as to the availability of the operation which had been denounced by the bishop!
Thus public advertising to back up person-to-person rumor was furnished by the very institution which was fighting the practice. A public discussion of sterilization in the spring of 1949 led to another pastoral letter. This one warned that a sterilized woman would not be admitted to communion, but it added, "unless she has sincerely repented." Thus the church seems to have made its adaptation to the requirements of the insular situation. Women in increasing numbers are seeking sterilization as the answer to their needs. Doctors in a position to judge estimate that in the past few years 60 per cent of all the women who have their children delivered in hospitals request that sterilization follow the birth.

This hasty summary of a complex question is based largely upon my own experiences on the island, partly as secretary of the Asociacion

OVERCOMING CULTURAL BARRIERS TO FAMILY LIMITATION

de Estudios Poblacionales, a non-governmental organization devoted to the study and discussion of population problems. Soon, however, we are to have an invaluable report on the social and psychological factors affecting fertility in Puerto Rico. It will contain the results of an "Indianapolis type" study carried on under the auspices of the Social Science Research Center of the University of Puerto Rico and the Office of Population Research of Princeton University, by Paul K. Hatt. Some 18,000 interviews were gathered, on an area sampling basis, and are now being analyzed. To the best of my knowledge, this will be the first such study outside our own culture and should be of tremendous value as a guide to further studies in other colonial and semi-colonial areas.[4]

The number of specific research projects which could be suggested are legion. What I believe we must seek is a shift of emphasis from the broad outlines of value systems and institutions to how people actually behave within those systems and institutions and how those who do not conform may be used to influence the remainder. There is a mine of information already available for desk study in the light of our needs on such matters as social change, social conflict, the impact of Western civilization upon the rest of the world, the growth of social movements, the emergence of "native" leadership, and the existing methods of population control (some control seems to be almost universal).[5] Field studies must supplement such efforts, especially those undertaken in connection with action programs. We need to apply, in as carefully controlled experimental situations as possible, techniques already worked out in other fields, e.g. the work of the National Research Council's Committee on Study of Changing Food Habits. Thus, I believe, we can make a substantial contribution to speeding social change in this critical field.

FUTURE COURSE OF RESEARCH IN FERTILITY

FOOTNOTES

1. Frank W. Notestein, "Problems of Policy in Relation to Areas of Heavy Population Pressure," in <u>Demographic Studies of Selected Areas of Rapid Growth</u>. New York, Milbank Memorial Fund. 1944. P. 151.

2. A valuable digest of materials on "Theoretical Aspects of Industrialization" by Wilbert E. Moore appeared in <u>Social Research</u>, Sept., 1948 (v. 15, no. 3), pp. 277-303.

3. The latter are dealt with in Marguerite N. King, "Cultural Aspects of Birth Control in Puerto Rico," <u>Human Biology</u>, Feb., 1948 (v. 20, no. 1), pp. 21-35.

4. This and other Puerto Rican population research is described in Kingsley Davis, "Puerto Rico's Population Problems: Research and Policy," <u>Milbank Memorial Fund Quarterly</u>. July, 1948. Pp. 300-308.

5. <u>Proceedings of the International Congress on Population and World Resources</u>, held at Cheltenham, England, August, 1948. London, Family Planning Association. 1948. 246 pp.; and Clellan S. Ford, <u>A Comparative Study of Human Reproduction</u>. New Haven, Yale University Press. 1945. 111 pp.

NEEDED RESEARCH ON FERTILITY OF NEGROES

Ira De A. Reid
Haverford College

We may begin a discussion of this subject by framing it within Bertrand Russell's classic statement that "ascertainable truth (thereon) is piece-meal, partial, uncertain and difficult." Ten years ago Pearl reported that[1] "all the evidence that has been accumulated by the work of the last quarter of a century on the subject agrees with cumulative force in showing that among civilized peoples of the western world the main factors leading to group or class differential fertility are environmental (non-genetic) in nature, and that any group differences in innate (biological) fertility, if they exist at all in such populations, play a small role in producing group differences in expressed fertility. With critically collected ad hoc material, . . . there does not appear to be any significant difference in innate fertility between whites and Negroes. . . . These results plainly imply that the differences between whites and Negroes in the United States in officially recorded birth rates are to be attributed primarily to differential environmental influences, and particularly to differences in the prevalence and effectiveness of the contraceptive efforts actually made in the two racial groups."

Lewis in The Biology of the Negro[2] accepts the interpretations advanced in such earlier studies as Holmes' The Negro's Struggle for Survival and in the analyses of Thompson, Whelpton, and Dublin. Kiser's[3] conclusions, derived from an analysis of the National Health Survey, indicate that "it appears unlikely that the low fertility levels and the high proportion of childlessness among urban Negro marriages are in any important part due to contraception. The inference may be drawn that lowered fertility, pregnancy wastage, and sterility in this group may be associated with venereal disease and history thereof. Since this is a problem with public health as well as population indications, the importance of specialized studies in this field is clearly apparent."

It is apparent, I think, that worth while research on the problems of central interest in the field of fertility is not routine, but a flexible and inventive process. It should be equally apparent that we have done little toward providing causal understanding of the phenomenon of fertility within the framework of "race" or color. A cursory examination of studies in this field reveals many strained ex post facto interpretations of differential fertility that do not fall within the design of good research. It is not apparent that existing findings in the field are adequate to answer either many crucial theoretical problems or important practical questions.

One of the chief recourses in our research on the fertility of Negroes has been what Max Weber called the "mental experiment," that is, when lacking the experimental control of the variables in fertility, we are forced to rely upon logical control by "wishing away" or "thinking away" one factor at a time in order to arrive at causal imputations. At best, this is a hazardous procedure. Not always has the method been employed by highly trained and mature scholars. The net result of this situation is that there has been no recent work on the fertility of Negroes; the second result is the impressions of most people— an impression not backed by scientific study— that a lowered fertility in Negroes is due in large part to the incidence of venereal disease, malnutrition, and such pathological conditions as myomata of the uterus, etc. Such an answer, however does not explain the high fertility of rural population as shown in crude birth rates. In addition, we only recently were asked to accept a conclusion based upon correlative but not causal evidence that the high rate of rejections of Negroes for military service was linked to the fact that a large proportion of the Negro population is born in areas where levels of living are lowest and health facilities and conditions are poorest.

All of this, it seems, indicates certain directions for research in the field of differential fertility as it relates to race and color. Assuming that we established a tenable and workable hypothesis in the Indianapolis study of fertility patterns of white couples, duplicate such a study for the "racial" community, giving due recognition to the need for specific definition of the terms of reference, to such factors as birth and marital fertility rates and, to age-specifics and pregnancy wastage controls. The medical schools of Howard University at Washington, D.C. and Meharry College at Nashville, Tenn. in cooperation with Fisk University would offer unique laboratories and bases for observing community and hospitalized samples of the urban populations by trained scholars in medicine, biology and the social sciences. Such a study would be useful, even if we wish to keep our present frame of racial reference, such terms as "native white," "Negro,"

NEEDED RESEARCH ON FERTILITY OF NEGROES

and "non-white."

A second suggestion is that there is need for a basic reexamination of the color-class categories used in demographic research as they relate to fertility data. In the analysis of such a biologically determined and socially modified factor as fertility it is questionable if the use of such categories can produce any data of scientific validity. An examination of the use of these concepts reveals a basic dualism. At the outset of a problem the terms "white" "Negro" or "non-white" may be used as <u>classificatory</u> structures, indicating more or less amounts of a single quality, in this instance, color. However interpretations of research data may reveal that at this point the concepts of color are being used as <u>substantive</u> structures, now implying the presence of separate and distinct identifiable characteristics presumed to be homogeneous. Furthermore, in our contemporary usage there is the implied assumption that a difference in bodily appearance is the crucial difference between color groups, and that these groups not only look different but <u>are</u> different. If the collected evidence indicates what it seems to suggest—that certain physical characteristics, in this instance color or "race," are not biologically significant but are socially significant because they are historically and culturally selected as symbols significantly differentiating between social groups—we need to use the available materials with extreme caution.

It is patently evident that there is no pure parent stock to be labeled white or Negro. What we have called <u>Negro</u> is apparently a congeries of primary parent stocks of many different strains. A rather basic study of reproductive behavior for example, could be made of mixed stocks and of relatively pure stocks, both of which are lumped as "Negro." Though for twenty years anthropometric data and reproductive behavior patterns concerning each of these categories (243 unions between whites and persons of Negro blood, and 1382 individuals representing stocks that are known to have been "pure" since pre-Civil war days) have been available in <u>A Study of Some Negro-white Families in the United States</u>[4] this basic framework has never been exploited in our demographic research. Frazier's studies of the Negro family[5] and Drake and Cayton's report on intra- and interracial mixtures in Chicago (<u>Black Metropolis</u>)[6] also suggest refinements that can be made in our basic research studies that will permit greater scientific validity in an analysis of the socially determined type called Negro.

At this point, therefore, our suggestions for research are broad ones: do we wish to continue explorations on fertility within the present

FUTURE COURSE OF RESEARCH IN FERTILITY

bifurcated framework of white and Negro? If so, would an experimental study along the Indianapolis study pattern provide significant comparable data? Secondly, have we reached an impasse in our color-linked analysis? Has the time come when we must reexamine and refine our basic concepts or tools as they relate to the color-race nexus— and restate them in terms of our present knowledge and requirements? Both theoretical expectations and research findings suggest that where we are relating our findings to socially visible physical differences, we need this refinement as a basic and ultimate prerequisite to understanding the true nature of the fertility of socially differentiated groups.

FOOTNOTES

1. Pearl, Raymond, The Natural History of Population. New York. Oxford University Press. 1939. Pp. 24-26.

2. Lewis, Julian H., The Biology of the Negro. Chicago. The University of Chicago Press. 1942. Pp. 11-13.

3. Kiser, Clyde V., Group Differences in Urban Fertility. Baltimore. Williams and Wilkins. 1942. Pp. 243-244.

4. Day, Caroline Bond. Peabody Museum of Harvard University, Cambridge. 1932.

5. Frazier, E. Franklin, The Negro Family in the United States. Chicago. The University of Chicago Press. 1939.

6. Drake, St. Clair and Horace R. Cayton. New York. Harcourt, Brace and Co. 1945.

THE FUTURE COURSE OF RESEARCH IN FERTILITY: MEASURES AND METHODS

Wilson H. Grabill
U. S. Bureau of the Census

The study of human fertility has advanced considerably during the past few decades. New measures, refinements of old ones, and various kinds of basic data have been developed. Contributions to our fund of knowledge have been made by many individuals and organizations with a wide variety of interests, as by physicians, economists, sociologists, and population analysts. The more we learn, the more new problems and avenues of research open up.

Reproduction rates — The subject of reproduction rates has been treated at an earlier point on the agenda of this meeting. At the risk of being repetitive, however, I should like to add a few words on the outlook for their further development, before passing on to other measures and methods.

I look for the continued wide-spread use of conventional reproduction rates despite their shortcomings and for the use, as supplemental tools, of any of a dozen or so refinements of those rates. For many countries, the conventional reproduction rates are the most that can be obtained at the present time, and the most that will be obtainable within the foreseeable future. These countries lack the materials needed for making adjustments of the basic data. Cost and other considerations make it unlikely that all countries can be persuaded to obtain the necessary detail. Many of the proposed refinements represent a substantial advance over conventional methods and they should be used wherever possible. However, these refinements have been and will continue to be tailor-made to fit the data available and the circumstances existing in each country. Variety will be the keynote.

It is neither possible nor advisable to take into account all factors affecting fertility when computing adjusted reproduction rates. A combination of certain factors may be optimum for one country but not for another.

FUTURE COURSE OF RESEARCH IN FERTILITY

For example, a method that relies heavily on births classified by legitimacy and by age at marriage by duration of marriage of the parents is not very suitable for countries where consensual marriages are common. No single method thus far proposed is altogether free from defects.

Among the types of research needed on reproduction rates are (1) studies which will indicate the approximate error in conventional reproduction rates, year by year; (2) studies to determine the optimum set of factors affecting fertility to be considered in adjusting rates for each country; (3) studies of the quality of the basic data, since undue refinement is not justified by poor data; and (4) continual research in an effort to improve existing methods.

<u>Distributional analysis versus rate analysis</u>— The kind of fertility analysis with which we are most familiar involves the use of rates of one kind or another, such as birth rates, reproduction rates, and even rates of young children. Aside from the work done by Woofter and Whelpton, there has been comparatively little accomplished in the way of published analyses of trends in the distribution of women by number of children ever borne. To illustrate, little publicity has been given to the trend toward 2 children as the modal number ever borne by women with completed fertility, to the trend toward the 1-child family in urban areas and the 3-child family in rural areas as secondary modes, and to the lack of any appreciable increase in the prevalence of childlessness among married women in recent decades. These distributional patterns are well-defined.

I am inclined to have little doubt that there is a limiting value below which the birth rate will probably not decline and also that there will be a virtual end to the spread of the small family system in this country within a few decades. However, we need more research along these lines, and more data on which to do the research than those available from the two censuses of 1940 and 1910. Rough trends are discernible from comparisons of data for successive age groups in a single census, but these are far less precise than those which could be made from observations for a number of dates. The trends inferrable from a single census are clouded by such things as differential mortality among women who have borne many children as compared with those who have borne few. Distributional analysis offers a promising avenue for the eventual sharpening of forecasts, and for many other projects.

<u>Related factors</u>— As you know, the Milbank Memorial Fund and the Scripps Foundation for Research in Population Problems have been

exploring for several years the field of social and psychological factors affecting fertility, through a special study of conditions among a group of native white Protestant couples in the city of Indianapolis. I am well pleased with the findings thus far. I would like to see more studies made along the same line. The original study has furnished much food for thought. Many of the aspects of the Indianapolis study cannot be repeated by the government. The government cannot ask some of the more highly intimate and personal questions. For that reason, I hope that the Population Association will encourage further research of this type by private persons and organizations. In the realm of measurement of sterility, a much needed control not thus far employed is the age at which the woman first tried to have a child. I have in mind the frequent conclusions that roughly 10 to 15 percent of married couples are involuntarily sterile, whereas census data indicate that, formerly, among many large groups of married women, only 2 to 4 percent never bore a child.

I anticipate more investigation into past trends in fertility as well as into future trends, with the use of new techniques or modifications of old ones, and the employment of data not heretofore used. There may even be a reduction in the emphasis on the role played by urbanization of the population as distinct from the role played by other developments in western civilization.

<u>Some plans for the 1950 census</u> — Our plans for the 1950 census are fairly well along. According to these plans we expect to have data again on women by children ever borne and by children under 5 years old. These data should provide the basis for an examination of how the high birth rates of recent years involved various population groups and produced temporary changes in the average number of children ever borne by women in these groups. New features may be (1) a special study of infant underenumeration and (2) some data on children under 1 year old, with conversions into estimated birth rates specific for age of the parents at marriage by duration of marriage by order of the child. From the study of infant underenumeration, we expect to learn more about the causes thereof and also obtain measures of the completeness of enumeration by social and economic characteristics, such as the educational attainment of the mother. These data, in turn, will enhance the use of data on young children for the study of differential fertility and may lead to procedural improvements in future censuses. A variety of reproduction rates will probably be worked out, many of them in cooperation with the National Office of Vital Statistics and using a combination of census data for bases and birth sta-

FUTURE COURSE OF RESEARCH IN FERTILITY

tistics in varying detail for numerators. More in the way of summary measures of differential fertility may be prepared with standardization for various factors. In brief, we hope for reports that will have greater value as compared with those for 1940, although they may not be as voluminous.

The National Office of Vital Statistics will again have a study of the completeness of birth registration. Improvement over the high level of birth registration attained in 1940 will probably be demonstrated. It is unlikely that, within the foreseeable future, the birth certificate can be modified so as to include new items such as age at marriage or duration of marriage. A special follow-up mail inquiry is being considered by the NOVS as a means of obtaining new kinds of data. Such a program would undoubtedly be on a sample basis. Certain practical problems would have to be solved before such a program could be carried out, however.

To sum up:
1. We may expect a variety of "adjusted" reproduction rates, each tailored according to the available data, and other unique circumstances in each country.
2. A method of "distributional analysis" may become nearly as popular as rate analysis as pertinent data develop.
3. New methods will be applied to past trends in fertility as well as to future trends, and there may be modifications in our philosophy as to the causes of the spread of the small family system.
4. Private foundations and persons should be encouraged to continue their investigations into such things as social and psychological factors affecting fertility.
5. Finally, a statement was made of some prospects from the 1950 census and from vital statistics in future years.

SOME ASPECTS OF RESEARCH IN DIFFERENTIAL FERTILITY

Ronald Freedman
University of Michigan

Although existence of fertility differentials between formal population categories is one of the best documented facts in the social sciences and although the measurement of fertility is probably more refined than that of any other social variable, few students of population are satisfied with existing knowledge in this field.

The kinds of social and economic categories available in census data are an important frame of reference for fertility analysis, but when they have been fully exploited a large part of the variation in fertility remains unexplained. Within occupational, educational, and income categories there remains a wide range of variation in fertility. It is clear that other kinds of social and psychological data are needed to account for fertility variation within the formal socio-economic categories. We cannot be satisfied with the socio-economic categories alone, even for the part of fertility variation they presumably explain. Most students of population predict the spread of the small-family pattern among the social classes. If this is true, then it is important to know what factors are distinctively linked to the small-family socio-economic categories.

The fertility deviant within each socio-economic category is particularly important for research. The small-family deviant in the high fertility socio-economic group should have characteristics deviating toward those of the low-fertility socio-economic category. The reverse should be true for the large-family deviant in the low-fertility category. Factors relating to fertility variations within the socio-economic categories should be a clue to factors lying behind the variations between the categories. The expectation is that fertility will be reduced in large-family socio-economic groups by a diffusion of attitudes now prevalent in the small-family socio-economic groups. Presumably, this diffusion has been in progress for some time, since family limitation is prevalent to some extent in every major population group in the United States. Therefore, it should be possible to study those persons in high fertility groups who have these attitudes as a test of the postulated effect on fertility and family planning. Exactly the reverse analysis should be possible for the socio-economic groups characterized by a small-family pattern.

This kind of approach does not involve abandoning the traditional socio-economic categories for fertility analysis. They are essential as a frame of reference for finding and testing other variables relating to fertility.

The kinds of data required for intensive analysis of fertility differentials within this framework are available from the Indianapolis Fertility Study. I would like to describe briefly plans for analysis of part of these data.

One kind of data available in the study consists of responses related to secular and rational social attitudes. The development of such attitudes in a scientific and urban civilization has been cited frequently as an explanation for the general decline in fertility and for differential fertility among socio-economic groupings. A strong theoretical case can be developed to support the view that a secular detachment from traditional values and a rational calculation of the consequences of behavior will lead to an increase in the rational planning of family size and a decrease in size of family planned. The Indianapolis data should give us one of the first empirical tests of this hypothesis with reasonably direct and adequate data.

Questions in the Indianapolis Study relating to traditional attitudes, religious practices and attitudes, and planning of personal affairs bear directly on the rational-secular hypothesis. The plan is to test the relationship within socio-economic categories between the secular rational indices on the one hand and the family-planning status and size of family on the other hand. If the secular-rational attitudes lead to effective planning and small families, such attitudes should be most prevalent among the low fertility groups who plan effectively. Further the families deviant in their own socio-economic groups with respect to family limitation practices should also be deviant with respect to these attitudes. It should be possible to make some evaluation of the effect of the spread of such attitudes among social classes. It may help to explain how formal population categories are related to fertility practices.

When the demographer goes behind formal census categories to relate such factors as secularism to fertility practices he might expect to find considerable help in existing sociological knowledge about the independent variables. Unfortunately, although there is a considerable body of helpful theory, there is little empirical data. In most cases the demog-

SOME ASPECTS OF RESEARCH IN DIFFERENTIAL FERTILITY

rapher cannot expect to hook up his refined measurements of fertility to established findings about the independent social and psychological variables. For example, in connection with the Indianapolis Study the by-product information about the relationship of religious practices and beliefs to socio-economic status will be a contribution to the general field of sociology as well as the taking-off point for fertility analysis.

The religious behavior variable is an excellent example of our inability to draw on existing conclusive knowledge as a starting point. In the Indianapolis Study we will be investigating the reasonable hypothesis that religious participation and belief are negatively related to family planning and positively related to size of family. Yet there is a considerable body of theory and some scattered evidence that the Protestant Ethic has accommodated to a secular-rationalism in personal behavior. At least on the surface this is inconsistent with the hypothesis. A preliminary resolution of the difficulty may be possible in the analysis. The data contain various indices of the nature of the religious participation (for example, whether related to theological belief, social-welfare approach, or purely social attractions). These religious indices may also be checked against data on traditional attitudes and on tendency to plan in general.

Another part of the Indianapolis data permits testing of several hypotheses about the effect of group memberships on fertility practices. In particular there are data on the characteristics of the individual's childhood family group and on his adult conformance to group patterns. The relationships of these group-influence indices to planning status and family size are to be analyzed within socio-economic categories, as in the case of the secular-rational variables.

Preliminary analysis plans concentrate on the separate relationships of each of the independent variables to the fertility variables. However, it will be possible later to study the interaction among those social and psychological factors most closely related to fertility. It is probably in the intensive analysis of configurations of factors behind the formal framework of census categories that we will attain our deepest understanding of the social aspects of human fertility.

An important feature of the Indianapolis data is the possibility of studying the effective planning of family size as the intervening variable between social and psychological factors and actual fertility. The present plan is to subclassify couples by "effectiveness of planning" before tabulations of the relationship between each particular social-psychological factor and fertility. The size of the sample does not permit the simultaneous study of relationships to family planning and fertility within socio-economic categories without some limitation of sub-classification. Therefore, for certain variables, it is planned to study within socio-economic categories the relationship of socio-psychological factors to fertility among those families which planned family size effectively. This group is homogeneous in contraceptive practice and reasonably large in size. This is a particularly crucial group, since it should illustrate the situation when the effect of other factors on fertility is not masked by variations in contraceptive practice. It is probable that for some time to come we shall have to concentrate on such "crucial experiment," "pure" groups in intensive fertility studies. The number of cases needed for complete analyses of the interrelationships of social factors, contraceptive practice, and fertility itself is probably prohibitive unless we concentrate on theoretically key groups of this kind.

In analyzing the relationships of social and psychological factors to the planning of fertility, it is planned to carry controls by socio-economic status throughout the analysis of the hypotheses described earlier in this paper. The use of this control will be more limited in the analyses of the fertility to which the planning leads.

Those of us who are working as newcomers in the analysis phase of the Indianapolis Study owe a great debt of gratitude to the group which formulated the plans for the study and carried through the considerable task of collecting and coding the data. The published description of the methodology of this phase of the study marks it as a model of careful research.

The considerable development of competent survey research organizations since the field phase of the Indianapolis Study makes it possible to suggest that future intensive fertility studies may be able to utilize their facilities for field work and coding. This will make it possible for population experts to concentrate their efforts in general study design and analysis. Such organizations as the Survey Research Center of the University of Michigan maintain an expert sampling section, interviewing staffs, and coding staffs which can handle the detailed field execution of a study more economically and quickly than a staff organized for a specific project. The technique of the open-ended interview developed in detail by the Survey Research Center is particularly appropriate for studies aiming at intensive analysis of attitudinal factors not easily obtained in short answer responses.

Another possibility is that of inserting a few questions relating to fertility in surveys being carried out by survey organizations in attitude areas believed to be related to fertility. The Survey Research Center has indicated its willingness to consider proposals for such by-product studies.

SOME ASPECTS OF RESEARCH IN DIFFERENTIAL FERTILITY

The added cost would be very small. Such surveys usually include questions on the formal socio-economic variables, so it should be possible to maintain the objective of keeping the intensive analyses of factors relating to fertility within the framework of existing knowledge of differential fertility.

THE PSYCHIATRIC APPROACH TO RESEARCH INTERVIEWING

Moya Woodside
Neurological Institute of New York

Our chairman has said that each paper in this panel holds a definite point of view, so I will state mine at the outset. In studies of factors affecting size of family, I believe that the qualitative small-scale inquiry is an essential supplement to the quantitative research more familiar to members of this conference. And furthermore, such inquiries should be undertaken by persons who have had some psychological training.

Someone, somewhere, once wrote: "All demographic trends are ultimately reducible to what happens in the bed." That is just what the research interviewer in fertility has to find out. How should it be done, who should do it, what should be their qualifications? As most of us know, while the itemised questionnaire or the doorstep interview may be adequate to obtain information on such things as — say — individual preference for radio programmes or breakfast foods, these methods are totally unsuited where the questions touch on involved personal and emotional reactions, inevitably associated with sexual and contraceptive behaviour. It is true that people in this country, compared with Britain, are franker about such matters — or possibly it is that they are more survey-conditioned. I certainly found it much easier to interview white Southern college graduates and Negro peasant women about sex than I did the lower-middle-class British housewife. But even granted that people are less superficially inhibited, there is still quite a long way to go.

It is now generally understood, I think, that the interviewer on this topic must be able to deal with sexual questions factually and unemotionally; that they should be led up to from a neutral introduction; and that all suggestion of "right" or "wrong" or "improper" be avoided (even tone of voice or a look is important here). The interviewer will also be forewarned of those common sources of error, coitus interruptus not being thought of as "birth control" and abortions being slipped in under the description of "miscarriage." But it is not enough to assume that when you select and groom your investi-

THE PSYCHIATRIC APPROACH TO RESEARCH INTERVIEWING

gator (perhaps a graduate student in college), see that he has read some of the literature, has an acquaintance with the vocabulary of contraception and sex practices, send him or her on a few trial interviews, and then expect to get adequate results. There is more to it than this, when you are dealing with a subject as emotionally charged as sex. The interviewer needs to know something of people, and to have an awareness of psychological mechanisms such as ambivalence, repression, rationalization, when he encounters them not in the text-book but in the individual. Experience of this sort cannot be imparted in a short training-course, however well-directed it may be.

I know that in this statistically-minded culture, graphs and tables and figures (if you get enough of them!) are often supposed to provide the answer to everything. But in fertility inquiries— assuming that we are interested in possibilities of modifying behaviour— <u>feeling</u> is as important as fact, attitudes as important as actions. The evidence we get will be distorted or inadequate, if we do not keep this in mind. Though one's "subject" co-operates in all good faith, he or she may be unable to free themselves of the inhibitions arising from their own inner conflicts (e.g., the woman who insists she is always careful over her contraception, yet has a series of unexplained "accidents"); or escape from giving the "approved" answers imposed by outer cultural standards (e.g., husbands in a London marriage inquiry[1] tended to say that such and such a baby had been "planned," whereas their wives, less influenced it seemed by social factors, would admit frankly that the pregnancy was an accident).

I feel strongly that the collection of statistics about human behaviour is only the beginning, not the end of our research. We need to understand what the experience <u>means</u> to the individual, if his responses are to be interpreted in their broader sociological context. Here it is that the other type of worker often employed in fertility interviewing, the public health or clinic nurse, falls short. Though it is usually simple for her to obtain the confidence and full co-operation of her patient or client in answering intimate questions, she is unable to see the social and psychological implications of the material collected. Without this interpretation and a relating to the culture, the data lacks much of its potential significance.

What should be the approach to the people we interview? Always we have to remember that they are not ciphers or anonymous "subjects," but they are human beings, each with individual personality make-up and an individual life situation. If we want them to talk to us, to reveal something more of themselves and their attitudes than appears on census sheets, we have first of all to be sincere ourselves, sincerely interested in them as persons, yet at the same time being alert to their reactions and their interview behaviour. I know that the research interviewer often feels like a scalp hunter, setting out each day to add a higher figure to his score! And that mindful of the essential statistical data which he must collect, he will endeavour to keep his quarry to the point with as few digressions as possible. But in research interviewing of this nature, concerned chiefly with attitudes, we will probably only get the information we want by allowing and even encouraging our "subject" to talk in what may seem an irrelevant manner about himself. The experienced observer sometimes picks up his most important clues from a chance remark, made in this way.

Let me illustrate this from a recent interview which I had in the outpatient clinic at Neurological Institute. There, as a matter of routine, the social worker sees everyone who is recommended for admission to the hospital and takes a brief social history, at the same time giving fuller particulars (where advisable) about their medical condition, probable length of stay in the hospital, etc., so that they can make immediate plans at home. The patient who came in to me on this occasion was a Negro woman, married and aged about 42, with a diagnosis of herniated disc. She was intelligent and co-operative, and we proceeded rapidly through the family and personal information which is required. She had been married for 20 years, but never had any children nor any pregnancies. I must have looked at her rather inquiringly, for she added (hastily, it seemed): "We just didn't want any."

Interviews in a neurological setting not being concerned with contraception or fertility, the conversation had to go on to other matters and I could only make a mental note of this remark. I later gave the patient such explanation as is usually adequate about her condition, and asked her if she were disturbed at the prospect of coming into the hospital for operation. No, she said, she had been suffering so much pain that she was prepared for anything that would bring relief. And here, normally, the interview would have ended, had I not noticed how tense she was and suspected that something was wrong. So I put away my pen and the case record, and encouraged her to talk about herself, what her husband was like, the work she did, etc. After a few minutes she suddenly started to cry, and then told me between her sobs that she was unhappily married, and that 10 years ago when she had become pregnant, her husband had compelled her to have an abortion. There were no physical ill-effects either then or subsequently; but nevertheless she was sure that her present condition was a direct result of this interference.

Always very religious, she had considered abortion a sin; and since taking ill, she had been haunted by these ideas of guilt and punishment which (till the interview) she had not dared to mention to anyone before. Well, it was not too difficult to reassure her and send her away feeling happier; but the point here is that unless the interviewer is aware of his subject's emotional state, important information may well elude him even though rapport is good and everything appears to be honestly answered.

There is also the question of how far the interviewer should press for information at the risk of spoiling a good relationship. Some would feel that the completed questionnaire, however reluctantly the material has been given, is what counts; and there is always the consoling thought, even if you are uncomfortable: "Oh well, I'll never see them again." Others, more psychiatrically minded, feel that questions which disturb and create anxiety should not be gone on with; and in any case, evidence so obtained is likely to be unreliable. Research interviewing should not be a ruthless process. It need not be, if the interviewer is prepared to respect the individuality of his subject, is skilled in establishing rapport, and—in this field—understands something of life as well as of sexual behaviour.

FOOTNOTE

1. <u>The Pattern of English Marriage</u> (provisional title), A Social and Psychiatric Study of Neurosis and Assortative Mating. Slater, Eliot, M.D., and Woodside, Moya. (in press).